D0462399

We Thought You Would Be Prettier

We Thought You Would Be Prettier

TRUE

TALES

OF

THE

DORKIEST

GIRL

ALIVE

Laurie Notaro

VILLARD

NEW YORK

A Villard Books Trade Paperback Original

Published in the United States by Villard Books,
an imprint of The Random House Publishing Group, a division
of Random House, Inc., New York.

VILLARD and "V" CIRCLED Design are registered
trademarks of Random House, Inc.

Library of Congress Cataloging-in-Publication Data

Notaro, Laurie.
We thought you would be prettier: true tales of the dorkiest girl alive /
Laurie Notaro.
p. cm.
ISBN 0-8129-6901-4
1. Notaro, Laurie.   2. Humorists, American—20th century—Biography.
3. Women—Humor.   I. Title.

PS3614.O785Z478 2005
813'.6—dc22   2004061179
[B]

Villard Books website address: www.villard.com

Printed in the United States of America
2 4 6 8 9 7 5 3 1

Book design by Jo Anne Metsch

To

Bruce Tracy and Jenny Bent;

Nana, whom I love so much it hurts;

and, naturally, that Mr. Hopkins

Contents

We Thought You
Would Be Prettier

Doing America

"Are you stupid?" the man behind the counter at the garage yelled at me. "Just how stupid are you? How could you be so stupid?"

Honestly, I just stood there, too shocked to say anything.

"Are you an idiot?" he asked, shaking his hand at me.

"Funny you should ask that," I said, trying to make a joke as I reached into my purse. "As a matter of fact . . ."

I slid the book across the counter toward him.

"What's this?" he asked, looking over the rim of his grimy circa-1970s glasses. "*Idiot Girls' Action-Adventure* . . . what? Club? Is that *Club*? You one of these idiots?"

"Yeah," I said and tried to laugh. "Pretty much. Guess you could say I wrote the book."

And to tell the truth, that was no lie.

In fact, I was only a matter of days into my book tour and I had already been called an idiot numerous times.

"I think if you get on a plane right now you're an idiot," my mother warmly informed me a week before my plane left for New York. "It's an ORANGE ALERT, you know. ORANGE. Orange isn't something to fool with! Fool around with yellow, green, or purple, but don't mess with orange! Because I'll tell you right now, if the orange terrorist gets on a plane, it's going to be the one you're on."

"I know," I said, trying to reassure her. "At least if it was the purple terrorist, he'd be easy to spot. He can sing 'I Love You' all he wants, but when that giant eggplant marches down the aisle, no one loves Barney if he's gonna be sitting in your row."

"You shouldn't be kidding around, you should be scared," my mother said, simply because *she* was.

"Scared?" I questioned bravely. "Listen, I've got a freckle on my arm that's changing colors more frequently than a Rainbow Brite, I have a tooth in the back of my mouth that's thumping louder than a stereo in a '79 Monte Carlo with a chain steering wheel, and either the zipper on the back of my sweater got bent at the dry cleaner's or I now have a neck hump the size of a bagel. I ran out of fear before I even left the house this morning."

But honestly, even I didn't believe myself.

Although I was determined not to let a silly old orange alert keep me from my long-awaited book tour, my mother had planted a seed. In fact, I had caught my imagination wandering about such an event. I had even choreographed scenarios in my head of lunging at the terrorist with a Vulcan grip and a swift kick where it counts. Then I would throw the weeping, bruised evildoer to the ground and shout, "You tell Osama Yo Mama to bring it on with the chicks who simultaneously have acne, gray hair, and suspicious moles, buddy! Because THAT is anger, Captain Cave, THAT IS ANGER!"

Suddenly, I look down and am dressed in a denim jumpsuit unzipped to my sternum, and behind me, Kate Jackson and Jaclyn Smith (please, don't talk Drew Barrymore to me—I was a teenager in the seventies and eighties, and as a result spent nearly a decade of my life with curling-iron burns on my ears, neck, and forehead, some of which matured into scars. Let me have my Farrah Fawcett dream—I have earned it) are ready to hand out free samples of Kickbutt Pie. Oh yeah, and my frosted, immaculately feathered hair ROCKS, making a majority of the other passengers visibly jealous. Now, despite the bravado of my Nick at Nite mind, I was days away from the date of my trip and I was trying very hard not to let my mother's words sink into my brain and nest there. Typically before a big trip I am so excited that I head to the airport days in advance, eating Cinnabons like a bear heading into hibernation. This time, however, I hadn't even started packing for the three-week-long trip.

I have to go, I told myself, it will be fun. This is your book tour! A trip around the country! Nice hotels, room service—that's right, *room service!* Cheesecake and wine at your command! You're going to *great* cities, I reminded myself—New York, Seattle, San Francisco, San Jose, Los Angeles, Ann Arbor. It's like being a rock star, well, without the rock, or the star, but still, you get to do America on your publisher's dime! And right now, it's not 117 degrees in any of those places.

But it is *where you live.*

And honestly, that alone was my inspiration to toss twenty-one pairs of underwear into the washing machine and then throw them into my suitcase. Once I realized that I could remove myself from a Phoenix summer—a place where a coin or safety pin left in the sun on a car seat for seven seconds becomes a glowing-red branding iron—for almost a month, I couldn't pack fast enough. I even packed a sweater in case I encountered a cold trend and hit temperatures under eighty-five degrees.

Now completely invigorated for my trip, I anticipated more security at the airport than usual due to the alert, and I was right. The security at the airport was heavier than the security at either of Madonna's weddings, but I was prepared and had arrived almost three hours before my scheduled departure.

What I was not prepared for, however, was my conflict with the metal detector, but I really don't believe that was my fault. See, the thing that was running through my head when I was getting dressed that morning was "comfort," not "Don't wear the pants that need a belt to keep them held up, because you just might have to take that belt off when you go through security. And when your wedding ring sets off the metal detector, the National Guard guy with the machine gun isn't really going to care that when you hold both your arms out to your sides—including the one that's clutching at your waistband—your pants will slide down to your fanny faster than a Kennedy getting off a bar stool after happy hour. He won't care, even if the hysterical, uncontrolled laughter from all two hundred people in line behind you drowns out any beep the little wand might make as it goes over your bra hook and the guilty wedding ring. He won't care. He's too busy being mesmerized by the old-grandma panties you're wearing, particularly the part where the white cotton separates from the elastic for about eight inches and forms what looks like a kangaroo pouch over the girth of your belly."

"What an idiot," I heard a man behind me say, and when I turned around I saw that he was shaking his head at me.

"Hey," I whispered to the National Guard guy as he patted my paunch. "See this guy behind me with no belt? I heard him say he used to golf with Jose Padilla!!"

As if that wasn't enough of a self-esteem buzzkill to last me for my whole tour, in a matter of hours I would find myself in a greasy, grimy New York City garage being called an idiot again by a guy with glasses so dirty they had turned green, a chip on his shoulder, and, directly underneath, armpit stains bigger than his head.

At least then, however, I was wearing a good percentage of my clothes.

2

Standing on the corner of Forty-ninth Street and Park in Manhattan, I was desperately trying to hail a cab. On *Sex and the City* hailing a cab is a piece of fat-free cake. All Sarah Jessica Parker needs to do is make a "Ta—" sound and, as if she just crossed her arms and nodded her head or wiggled her nose, a taxi comes rolling to a stop merely inches away from her sixty-four-pound body, which is draped in transparent clothes, most likely involving knickers and a tube top fashioned from Cling Wrap.

It's a snap.

At Forty-ninth and Park, however, Sarah Jessica was not hailing a cab; I was, and I wasn't exactly having the luck of a fictional, fabulous, gorgeous television character. In the first place, once my hair met the humidity of New York City, I looked as if I was answering a casting call for a revival of *Godspell*. The hair that I have trouble controlling in the dry, arid desert had now exploded and grown, expanding to such unnatural proportions that I kept seeing this big brown cloud following me out of the corner of my eye. I kept thinking that New York had a desperate pollution issue until I realized that the thing blocking out the sun was my very own head. No one had warned me to bring the necessary hair-care products, but honestly, looking back on it now, I think the only thing that would have prevented my hair from becoming airborne was furniture paste or a net, like the ones dolphins get caught in.

Not having good looks to bank on—now, granted, hailing a taxi isn't like hitchhiking, where flashing a leg and a bit of cleavage will certainly help you get from Orlando to Branson on fifteen bucks and a pack of GPC Lights—I was at a major disadvantage, because when faced with the choice of steering a vehicle toward Sarah Jessica Parker or Arlo Guthrie in a dress, who are you going to pick? Picking someone up in a taxi isn't a marriage proposal, certainly, but when it comes to checking out the eye candy or the eyesore in the rearview mirror, well, I lose before the cards are even dealt.

Finally, when all of the more attractive, wealthier-looking people hailing a cab on Park were picked up, a straggler from the taxi herd thankfully took pity on me and pulled over. He was a husky, silver-haired, bulbous-nosed man eating a sandwich with excessive mayonnaise on it, but I hardly had room to be picky.

"Vertigo," he grunted in what I understood to be a thick Eastern European accent as I plopped myself into the backseat, which smelled like a deli that had been shut down by the city health inspector.

"I'm sorry?" I said, trying to breathe through my nose.

"VERTIGO," he said louder, and this time shook his hand toward me.

I shook my head. I had no idea, although I was about to inform him that as a passenger, I had the right to a clean taxi that did not smell like a storage unit for dried, salted meats, as well as an English-speaking driver, and, if Mr. Salami needed reminding, I would be more than happy to pull out the Passenger Bill of Rights that I had received from the taxi monitor at JFK and show him precisely where he was in violation.

Instead, Mr. Salami yelled at me again, "VERE TO GO?"

"Oh," I replied with relief and a chuckle. "Oh! I thought you were talking about the movie, or got the translation for 'car sickness' wrong."

Mr. Salami just stared at me. He did not chuckle.

"Fifty-first and Eighth," I delivered quickly.

Six minutes later, I was at the corner of Fifty-first and Eighth. Remembering my mother's words of caution, apart from her Orange Alert advice, I felt for my wallet before I got out. "You're going to get mugged. Count on it. I'm a New Yorker. I know. Don't look up at the tall buildings, everyone will think you're an asshole and then they'll mug you because of it. Keep your hands on your wallet at all times, unless you're getting mugged, and when you do finally meet your muggers, just hand it over. Muggers are very sick individuals. Give them what they want. Unless it's dirty and depraved, that's something you just can't come back from. And keep your driver's license someplace different. If a mugger takes it, you'll never get on another plane without it. It's an Orange Alert, you know."

With my hands reassuredly feeling my wallet in my purse, I got out of the cab and then quickly remembered to ask for a receipt.

Mr. Salami grunted again and then tore it off the meter.

He was almost out of sight when a little, nasally maternal voice in a New York accent inside my head told me to feel for my wallet one more time, just to be sure. So I did, and I felt it again, breathed a sigh of relief, then pulled it out to prove it to myself.

In my hand was my cell phone inside the cell-phone case that my husband had bought me especially for this trip after he gave my phone a "tune-up," which, I'd just noticed, was of about the same size and feel as my wallet.

My wallet was gone. Absolutely gone.

I suddenly felt as if my stomach had been quickly sucked out of my body by an Electrolux.

"*Your wallet is gone?*" my agent Jenny screamed as I stumbled through her office door. "Oh my God, you'll never be able to get on another plane. It's an Orange Alert! You have five more cities to go to!"

"I know," I said, still stunned. "All I really want to do right now is throw up or cry. I can't decide which one to do first."

"Where is the last place you had it?" Jenny asked.

"In Mr. Salami's cab," I said. "I'm thinking I should throw up first and *then* cry. This way, when I start to hyperventilate, there's no danger of a Jimi Hendrix–like death."

"Did you get a receipt?" Jenny said, and I nodded and handed it over. "Thank God. Now at least we have the medallion number of the cab. I'll call the taxi commission now."

When Jenny finally got through to the dispatch office, they said they would try to find Mr. Salami but that the chances of getting my wallet back were little to none. Who knew how many other fares he had picked up after me, any of whom could have helped themselves to it.

I didn't know what to do. I had no money, no credit cards, no bank card to get more money, no ID, and no hotel key card.

I had lost my wallet in New York City, and without any assistance from a mugger, robber, pickpocket, or thief. My mother gave me a lot of credit, I thought to myself. She never even entertained the possibility that I would end up simply mugging myself.

I was stupid. I was broke.

I was stranded.

So I threw up.

3

With no money, no credit cards, and no ID, I began to see New York City as a very ugly place. All of a sudden, I felt like the little match girl, lost and alone, and was sure that at any moment my clothes would begin to unravel with wear, my face would look as if I just stepped out of a coal mine, and I would begin speaking with a Spice Girl accent.

After having watched my wallet drive away in the backseat of what was essentially a sausage on wheels, I was at a definite disadvantage. I was only on the first stop of my book tour and had essentially caused it to come to a screeching halt.

While my agent Jenny manned the phone, trying to find the

right taxicab company to locate the MIA wallet, I decided to walk back to my hotel and explain the situation to get another key card so I wouldn't have to deal with that whole mess after my reading that night.

I was about to cross the street when I heard a strange noise—a digital, muffled, robotic melody of sorts—and then the traffic sign flashed WALK. The melody repeated a number of times as I entered the crosswalk, and then stopped just as suddenly as it started. No one else seemed to be paying it any mind, so I didn't either, and just kept walking.

I was waiting for the light to change at the next block when I heard the very same robotic melody again, and as I crossed the street, it seemed to just vanish. I looked at the people around me, but I didn't see anyone else looking like they were wondering what the jaunty little tune was, so I thought, This just must be a New York thing. One of those little oddities, like dirty men peeing out in the open, and roasted peanuts you can eat right off a wagon. It's New York. You get your horror and you get your snacks when you least expect them. On the next block, I stopped and waited for the little song before I crossed, but in vain. Silence. Nothing. Not even a note.

One block up, however, I was rewarded as the chipper little melody floated through the air, and as I stepped off the curb, I suddenly had a thunderbolt of revelation: The tune was a Safe Crosswalk Song for Blind People! Simply amazing! That Rudy Giuliani, he thought of everything! What other city could boast playing whimsical, frisky little melodies at busy intersections so that those deprived of sight could cross safely and have their spirits boosted at the same time?

I was still marveling at this new discovery when I entered my hotel, where despite my having checked in less than four hours earlier, no one remembered me, and therefore they declined to give me another key to my room without my ID, or at least something with my name on it.

"I know why you don't remember me!" I said, trying to jog their memories. "When I came in, I had regular hair, not *Welcome Back, Kotter* hair."

Then, suddenly, in the middle of my pleading, I heard the familiar notes of the Safe Crosswalk Song for Blind People. That's odd, I thought. Is there a Blind Person Xing somewhere in the lobby? I looked around, thinking that was erring a little too far on the side of safety as far as I was concerned, when the hotel check-in girl who didn't remember me looked me in the eye and said drolly, "Are you going to answer that?"

I must have given her an odd look, because then she emitted a deep, disgusted sigh and said, "That's coming from *you*. That's your phone."

I fumbled in my purse for a second, protesting that no, my ring is the basic ring the phone comes with, I don't know how to change those things, only my husband would—yes, yes, yes!—the very same husband who got me the cell-phone case and gave the phone his own brand of "tune-up." As in charging the battery, programming in numbers, and, apparently, changing my ring.

I pulled the phone out of its case and before I could even say hello, I heard Jenny scream on the other end, *"Where have you been? I've been calling you every three minutes! Get back here now! They found your wallet! The guy at the dispatch garage is waiting for you!"*

I ran back to Jenny's office, where she gave me a twenty and an address and shoved me into another cab.

I found the garage, a grimy little cavern in the heart of Hell's Kitchen. Now, it wasn't as if I expected Tony Danza and Danny DeVito to come out, greet me, and invite me to join them in a round of cards, but the last thing I expected was a shout coming from deep within the shadows of the cab cave directed unmistakably at me.

"You the one? You the one with the wallet?" the disembodied Wizard-of-Oz-via-the-Bronx voice said.

"Yeah," I nodded, walking into the garage.

"Are you stupid?" the voice, now clearly belonging to a man standing behind a counter, yelled at me. "Just how stupid are you? How could you be so stupid? Are you an idiot?"

Do you know my mother? I wanted to ask him.

"You gotta be an idiot to do what you done," he said as he pulled my wallet out of a drawer and plopped it on the counter.

"Listen," I told him, "I already know that I'm an idiot, but I'm on my first book tour, this is my first stop, and I have the rest of the country to do. If I didn't get this wallet and my ID back, I wasn't going anywhere."

"Of course not," he replied as he scoffed. "It's an Orange Alert!"

"Really?" I said, trying to smile. "But what I'm trying to say is that I cannot thank Mr. Sal—the very kind cabdriver enough for bringing this back. It's more important than it seems."

"Well, it *seems* that the cabdriver lost out on a seventy-buck fare to JFK when he decided to turn around and bring this back," the dispatcher said. "It *seems* that way."

"Well, I'd like to give him a copy of my book in appreciation," I said with a big smile.

"I'm sure he'll love that," the dispatcher said dryly. "That will almost make up for the seventy bucks *plus tip* that he lost to make sure you could go on your trip."

I nodded, smiled tightly, and pulled a wad out of my wallet.

"Twenty, forty, sixty, seventy, seventy-five, seventy-six, seventy-seven, seventy-eight, and I'm keeping this ten for cab fare back," I said. "Is that enough appreciation?"

"Seems that way," he said. "But you can take your book."

"Thanks," I said as I gathered up my stuff, including my book, and headed out.

"Hey, Idiot Girl!" the dispatcher called out to me as I was almost to the sidewalk. "Hang on to that wallet, okay?"

"Are you kidding?" I laughed back. "I'm on *Red* Alert."

4

I am not a giant.

I'm not tall, I'm not statuesque, I'm not lanky. I'm short and squat, like a molar. If I were a form of foliage, I would not be an alpine or redwood, I would be a rhododendron or kudzu. I'm a shrub. A succulent, perhaps. I'm a barrel in human form. I am quite nearly a midget among men.

Still, when the seat in front of me suddenly lurched backward and almost into my lap as I was crammed into a teeny-tiny seat that only a newborn could find accommodating on my flight back from New York to Seattle, I was absolutely furious.

I was at a loss for words during this instance, because in the first place, BECAUSE IN THE FIRST PLACE, how can reclining your seat back an inch and three-quarters make any kind of difference in comfort unless you are bleeding profusely from the head? How can it? It simply can't, especially if you don't have a footrest kick up at the same time or someone to plop a frosty one in your hand and a bowl of onion dip in your lap. An inch and three quarters, however, is enough of a dent in my space to make things more cramped than a marathon runner with a potassium deficiency. Because a one-and-three-quarters-inch bite all across the board was a significant percentage when I only had about six inches of personal airline space to begin with. And you know, if I can be frank, if I didn't care about that inch and three quarters, I would have hit Cinnabon, Pretzel Mania, CPK, Paradise Bakery, and Margaritaville in a rampant, maniacal carbohydrate binge before I boarded.

So see, I cared. I cared about that inch and three quarters, which if you multiply it by the 17.2-inch width of the standard seat, equals 21.35 inches, which in my book, is a BIG HUNGRY MAN-SIZED BITE out of my personal airline space. It's as big as a baby!

And this was all compounded by the fact that the woman in front of me, the woman who had decided to steal my space by choosing to recline, was the size of a circus peanut. You could cram her and twenty-three members of her family into a Crayola box. I know this because I saw her at check-in and remarked to myself that someone was playing with a Lord Farquad puppet/marionette and wondered where they got it because I wanted one, until I realized it was a real-life little lady. And now here she was, all annoying two feet of her, reclining very confidently into my lap while her feet weren't even touching the floor. Personally, I think reclining needs to be outlawed, because what the passenger in front of me takes for himself he takes away from me. I have paid for that space. In retaliation, I believe seats should be fully equipped with a GUESS AGAIN, LA-Z-BOY!! button on the back side of every headrest to automatically shoot these space suckers back into the upright position. Or, at the very least, there has to be some sort of consent document signed by both parties involved in the recline in order for that action to take place. If no such agreement has been made, then the person being reclined upon has the complete and total right to make a citizen's arrest or to exact some form of physical retribution.

I mean, honestly, I wasn't really all that much bigger than Miss Lord Farquad, but I needed that space, and I got so angry that

I started searching frantically through my complimentary airline snack mix for a sharp corn chip or broken pretzel that I could throw at her. I figured if something like that could almost kill a president, I might have some chance of doing damage to my recliner. I finally found a rice snack the approximate shape of a spear head, and as I was about to shoot it toward her tiny pea skull, a burst of turbulence knocked it out of my hand and onto the ground. I had to uncross my legs to get it, a maneuver that should strictly be confined to an intermediate-to-advanced yoga class, but as a result, I discovered the recliner's mortal enemy: The Kicker.

Funny, it seems as though she liked having her kidneys beat on like they were a set of bongos at a Jimmy Cliff concert as much as I liked studying her female pattern baldness while her coconut head was in my lap.

Next time, though, I'm saying "yes" to Cinnabon and getting seconds on the Mexican food, too, just in case I need backup.

And I mean backup.

5

"*That's* the way you're going to sign your book?" my sister said, completely aghast one night at a family dinner right after the book had been released. I had just finished signing a copy for her friend, who I felt sure was going to try and sell it on eBay. "That's just your name! You can't do that! There's no flash, no pizzazz! No one is going to wait in line for a dumb old signature like that! I had fancier signatures in my high school yearbook!"

"Well, I guess I could add, 'Stay sweet!' or '2 Good 2 Be 4 Got 10' or 'Have a bitchin' summer, dude,' " I said. "Or I could embellish my signature by dotting my i's with clouds or hearts for full fancy potential."

"I've really given this some thought, and if I were you," my father piped in, "I'd sign it, 'Thanks for being a fan.' I think people would appreciate that."

I smiled and I nodded, but honestly, it sounded a little weird to me. "Thanks for being a fan, Laurie." It felt kind of, well, maybe patronizing, presumptuous, and even a bit snobby, to tell the truth. It didn't sit well with me at all. Danielle Steel has fans, I reasoned, J. K. Rowling has fans, I concluded. But me? *Fans?* That's just ridiculous and asinine, I told myself, not to mention laughable. I don't have fans, I simply have more potential drinking partners, although on this tour I barely had time to take advantage of it.

In fact, going on a book tour wasn't what I had imagined going on a book tour would be. Essentially, it went like this: I would get off a plane, grab a taxi to the hotel with my hand on my wallet the whole trip, and have enough time to take a peek inside the minibar to decide between an eighteen-dollar jar of dry roasted peanuts and a four-dollar year-old Toblerone bar before my escort showed up to drive me to numerous "drop-ins." "Drop-ins" are exactly that, dropping into a bookstore and signing whatever number of copies may be on hand, although sometimes the visit involved sales associates who appeared visibly very angry that I was delaying their break, or a glitch in the computer system that denied my claim as a writer and my book entirely, or a harried scream from an overprotective employee demanding to know why I was scribbling in her books and that I should stop immediately because she had just called security. Then, typically, I'd go back to the hotel room, wash my face while my poor escort was circling the block, get back into the car and go to a reading, sign some more books, and then go back to the hotel, where I'd pack and get ready to be at the airport in the morning.

If this was a tour, I wondered, where were the buffets backstage? In fact, *where* was backstage? Backstage, in my case, essentially translated to "that corner behind Self-help and Gay Interest," and believe me, the only food back there was stuff that Overeaters Anonymous members had dropped by mistake. I mean, I saw *Almost Famous*. I *know* what a tour is supposed to be like! And here I was on a *tour* and I never once got to proclaim myself a "Golden Goddess" and jump off a roof, I didn't get to trade a groupie for a case of beer, and my escort never had the whimsy or bravado to bust through the gates of a Barnes & Noble, not even for my delight. The most exciting thing that happened was that I figured out how to order pay-per-view in my hotel room and I left some towels on the floor. What was I doing wrong? I thought to myself, and then it hit me. Sure, I was on tour, but I wasn't the singer, guitarist, or even the bass player from *Almost Famous*. I was *the little kid*. The boring little writer. The boring, tired little writer, and sometimes cranky if the minibar didn't offer me a wide enough balance of sugary and salty snacks.

I found this out the hard way in Seattle when I was getting ready "backstage." (I decided to adapt the restroom into my own personal lounge before my "show." Well, not the *whole thing*, just one stall.) I had scarfed down my sixth Toblerone of the tour a couple of hours before for dinner and was suffering from heartburn. All of a sudden, while I was in my lounge, there was Ian Astbury, the lead singer of the Cult, singing "Fire Woman" to me and pelting me with gummy bears. Then, oddly enough, Ian Astbury, now a monkey, was trying to look up my dress and snap my girdle—I mean, body shaper. "Hey," I yelled at the monkey, shaking my leg, "that is not cotton, the fabric of our lives, you know! You just gave me Spandex Burn!"

That's right, I had fallen asleep while sitting on the "chair" in my "lounge," a wonderful little spot where all of my insecurities could gather in a dream and torment me. Frankly, I don't know how long I was out, but when I finally got off the toilet and stumbled out to the reading, I had crease lines on my face from where my cheek got all bunched up like drapes from being pinned against the bathroom wall.

Now, fortunately and unfortunately, sometimes people from your past find your reading at the local bookstore a very opportune time to reconnect in front of a bunch of strangers. This is great when it's someone you have missed; it's not so hot in front of twenty to thirty attendees when the guy who sat next to you in macroeconomics in 1991 puts you on the hot spot with the "What's my name?" game, and is acting as if you did more one Thursday night than group-study for a midterm.

For the most part, however, I was happy to reconnect with old, dear friends who have relocated to other parts of the country, as was the case when I walked with my wrinkled face to the podium in a Seattle bookstore. I looked down into the crowd and there was my dear, dear friend Parker, whom I hadn't seen since he moved to the Pacific Northwest with my once-close friend Jack, who was conspicuously not there next to Parker.

I knew why. Jack and I had started a magazine together almost a decade before. It got off to a good start, but after a year or so the publication was struggling and tempers were flaring. Our once happy staff—a group of tightly knit friends—was torn into two camps: the group that wanted to ride out the storm and see how far we could take the magazine we had built, failing if we had to; and the group that wanted to raise ad revenue by allowing some more-than-slightly-distasteful advertising and content in.

One day Jack came into the office and, being the editor, fired everyone in the opposing camp. It was a devastating blow, the closest thing I had felt to a divorce, and I packed up my things and left. We had not spoken or seen each other since he gave me my walking papers. That was that. The magazine published two, maybe three more issues, and then, despite the unsavory ads, absolutely sank.

After the reading, Parker came up to me with two books in his hand—one for himself, he said, and one for Jack.

"I called him all day to get him to come," Parker tried to explain. "But he said he's at work on a deadline and couldn't make it."

And then we both laughed.

"He's still in magazines?" I asked, to which Parker nodded. "Which one?"

"Oh, it's called *Hot Cherry*," Parker said. "Porn."

I signed Parker's book, told him how much I missed him, and then he handed me the one for Jack.

I sat there for a moment, thinking, thinking, thinking. And then I knew.

"Dear Jack," I wrote on the title page, "Thanks for being a fan."

6

I was trapped. Trapped at a crowded airport gate. People were sprawled, moaning, screaming, running, yelling, everywhere. From above, I'm sure the vision resembled a scene from a 1970s disaster movie.

I couldn't move without touching somebody, and I don't like that. I had waited for three hours for the plane to arrive that would take me from Seattle to San Francisco, and frankly, if I had been wearing more comfortable shoes, I could have hoofed it and gotten there faster. At least it would have been more enjoyable than being crammed into a gate with my laptop, an elderly woman, and approximately two hundred members of the same Japanese high school basketball league.

Teenagers. Hundreds and hundreds of them. They looked like locusts. Buzzing all around, creating havoc and mayhem. When the first group initially arrived at the gate, I found them cute and adorable. They all had matching shirts and luggage, they were all so cheerful and loaded with boundless energy. Some of the girls had pigtails. They giggled. They laughed. They played games.

"Hoti hoti hoti, yoti yoti yoti, seen a seen a so," some girls in a corner sang in Japanese—granted, my transliteration is rather rough. In time with their tune, they clapped their hands rhythmically along, playing some sort of game.

I smiled, thinking back to my own high school trips, except that my hair wasn't as shiny and bouncy as theirs, and we didn't play clapping games, we just got drunk.

"Seen a seen a so," I sang in my head.

Then another group from the same league arrived at the gate, and stuffed their luggage, duffel bags, and random, loose basketballs in among the empty chairs.

Their chatter grew louder, more girls joined the clapping game behind me, but hey, I thought, they're kids. Let them have their fun. They're just having fun.

"Hodi hodi hodi," the girls sang, beating their quick little hands together.

When the third group shuffled in, things started to get a little tight. And they got a little louder. And it started getting hot in that gate because the amount of energy that two hundred Japanese high school basketball players can generate was enough to put a silly old split atom to shame.

A basketball zoomed by my head. They were playing catch. Someone stepped on my foot. The noise level boomed. There was nowhere to walk. It was getting very hot. It was hard to breathe.

"HODI HODI HODI!!!" the girls screeched like chimpanzees behind me.

My God, when is that plane going to get here? I thought as my fingers rubbed my sweaty, throbbing temple, but then I remembered that the plane getting here wasn't going to solve anything, because *they were all on it.*

THEY WERE ALL ON IT.

"SEEN A SEEN A SO!!!!"

Oh God, I moaned to myself, this is a nightmare! This is a complete nightmare! None of their coaches was doing anything to rein these basketball maniacs in because they had apparently been worn down to human nubs by these teenage monsters. I saw their chaperones, and what remained of them were just shells, ravaged to the bone. Some of them were actually sleeping during all of this from exhaustion. Either that or they had probably just died.

I was trapped in an anime movie.

It was horrible, especially when I had the realization that if my plane went down—I mean, it *was* an Orange Alert—the headlines wouldn't cry YOUNG (SUBJECTIVELY SPEAKING) AUTHOR'S PROMISING LIFE SORROWFULLY CUT SHORT, but TEEN JAPANESE BASKETBALL LEAGUE DECIMATED IN HARROWING AIR TRAGEDY, and then maybe, if I was lucky, a subhead might read: BARELY WORTH MENTIONING CRANKY WRITER DIES, TOO, ALTHOUGH BASKETBALL TEAM DEATHS ARE OBVIOUSLY WAY SADDER.

All I ever wanted was for my fiery death to be a full story, and now, all I was going to be was a sidebar.

"HODI HODI HODI!!!"

Even now, I am amazed that I survived the ordeal, amazed that I did not run to the food court and try to stab myself to death with a plastic fork and take one or most of the clapping girls with me.

When we finally landed in San Francisco, I met my escort, Grania, at the airport entrance. She was a wonderful, sweet woman who noticed my distress and gave me the last column of a Kit Kat bar she had left over from lunch. We did our drop-ins, went to the hotel, then headed out to San Jose for the reading that night. After spending two and a half hours on the freeway to go fifty miles, we finally arrived at the bookstore for that night's reading.

I was exhausted, still had my Japanese Teen Basketball headache, and all I really wanted to do was find a nice stall "backstage" and hunker down for the winter. My mission was interrupted by a young girl who worked at the bookstore and was running the event because her boss had abandoned his post and left her in charge. Which was not a good thing, mainly because she was green.

"You don't look so good," I told her. "Are you okay?"

"I had my wisdom teeth pulled yesterday," she explained as her skin got greener by several shades and she broke out into a heavy sweat. "I didn't have to go to school today, but my boss called me in."

"Are you at Berkeley?" Grania asked.

"Oh, no," she replied, holding on to a table to keep herself up. "I'm a junior in high school, and I thought if I came in it would show my boss that I was dedicated and might advance my career in the company."

"This is what I think," I said point-blank. "You need to go home, pop some Vicodin, go suffer in your own bed, and apply at Dairy Queen when your head swelling recedes a bit so it's not so . . . circus size. Any boss that would make you come in to work is a guy you need to tell to kiss your grits."

"Okay," the little green girl said weakly.

"And go to college! Graduate, come back, and show that joker how to run this store!" I said quickly, being that her eyes glazed over and were fluttering to stay open. "Oh boy. I know that look. That's a throw-up face."

"I just need to sit down," she said, plopping into one of the seats set up for the reading as Grania offered to get some water for her.

I, in turn, took this opportunity to go "backstage" and go over some notes before the reading started. And that's just what I was doing in my own private little stall, when, suddenly and without warning, I heard a trumpet blow.

Oh dear Lord, I thought to myself and tried really hard not to laugh at the person who had done it.

Until I realized it *had come from me.*

Oh no, I thought to myself, I hate it when that happens. I hate it when one little bubble gets ahead of the pack and simply can't wait to get out and see what's on the other side without a permission slip.

With only minutes to go before the reading started, I reluctantly got my stuff together and left the stall, and smiled at the lady washing her hands at the vanity. She smiled back, too, but a smile that said, "So it was you, huh? Now I can put a face to the fart."

It was a very uncomfortable few seconds for me until she finally finished up and left, leaving me feeling ashamed, embarrassed, and also not quite so bloated. I dried my hands and headed out to the reading.

"Are you ready?" the green girl said, to which I nodded, but as soon as I saw rows and rows and rows of empty chairs, I didn't feel quite so enthusiastic. Aside from the green girl, aside from Grania, there was only one other person in the audience. Only one person had come to my reading. Only one lady.

And she was the very one who had heard me blow the trumpet merely moments before.

Now, honestly, I'm not sure which of our expressions best exemplified the look of naked horror, mine or hers, but for the next half hour, I couldn't go anywhere and she couldn't go anywhere. We were both prisoners, held there by the glue of mortification and not knowing what else to do. I mean, I couldn't even look anywhere else but at her, she was *the only person there,* and she couldn't look at anyone else but me, and there we were, for thirty long, torturous minutes, locked in this unpleasant, suffering circumstance until the green girl wandered over and announced, "My painkiller is wearing off, I'm going to call my mom to come get me."

And when it was over, when I called it a day at that very moment and freed my one unfortunate audience member, letting her go forth into the world never to forget the most ghastly, appalling half hour she had spent in her life, quite thankfully, no one clapped.

7

I guess a tooth can just fall out of your head at any time. You never know. You could just be nibbling on a roll in a restaurant, waiting for your dinner to arrive, when all of a sudden, there's a tooth in your napkin.

And I happened to know that pretty darn well, because there I was in Los Angeles an hour before my reading, looking at my tooth in my napkin.

Now, to be fair, what I was looking at was a crown, the brand-new $800 crown my dentist had just fitted me with before I left for my book tour. Some people don't really consider crowns as teeth, but let me tell you, when bad genetics and lazy flossing have their way with you, you're happy to consider anything in your mouth pale in color and harder than chewing gum a tooth. To be truthful, however, I was not looking at a pale tooth but a gold tooth, I suppose because my dentist has what I would now classify as a "skewed" sense of humor. Apparently, he took advantage of the fact that while under the gas I was higher than Courtney Love gets minutes before a court date then he saw fit to install things in my mouth that were sparkly, pretty, and had a far higher profit margin than a regular old porcelain job.

"What did you do?" I said when I finally came to and caught a

glimpse of the gold tooth in the hand mirror provided by my mad-man dentist. "You put bling in my mouth! Look at me. I am BLING-ING. I'm going to have to sell my regular-person car and buy an Escalade now, you know."

As I held the key to my rap/hip-hop career in my hand, I thought to myself, What are these things held in with, Scotch tape? I mean, I have nightmares about stuff like this, sure, but really, unless I was involved in a union brawl or went to live in a trailer park, I never expected to be able to spit a molar out of my mouth and into my palm.

My dinner arrived, but unless, as I told my waiter, he could find a way to make a chicken parmigiana into an ice cream float, I was gonna take a pass. Plus, I didn't really have time to worry about the hole in my mouth; I had a reading to get to in about twenty minutes. I figured that if I stuck a wad of chewing gum into the nub that my crown used to fit over, I could somehow protect it and I would not be so horrified about the fact that I essentially had a Tic Tac for a tooth.

And the gum worked, I was surprised to find out, it really did. It worked as long as I kept my mouth closed and didn't speak. Which, for an author about to conduct a reading stretching any-where from an hour to several, wasn't an ideal position. You see, once I started the reading, the gum fell off during the first para-graph I read, and feeling rather uncomfortable sticking my hand in my mouth to keep the gum tacked down, I simply swallowed it. Much to my dismay, however, even though my tooth was gone, jagged, sharp chunks of the cement that really hadn't fulfilled its duty to keep it there remained, slicing the side of my tongue when I attempted to talk.

Despite that, I would like to think that the reading had been going well; it was an intimate crowd, about five, maybe seven peo-ple, not big enough to warrant the PA system that had been set up, but still, small can be good. We were doing okay. So far, I had managed to swallow the blood leaking from my ripped and shredded tongue as I lapsed deeper and deeper into a lateral lisp, and, at this point, no one was complaining.

Until *they* came.

I saw them as soon as they rolled in, coming toward our small little contented group. The pair, an elderly man and woman, both in wheelchairs, made their way down the long aisle, spotted us, and then headed straight for my group.

Eventually, they took two spots in the "back," which, considering the small size of the audience, was about four feet from me. They both leaned in, cupped their ears like I've seen my Nana do, and began to listen.

Well, sort of.

"Wha?" the man sort of yelled. "Whatchoo saying? We can't—can't hear a word!"

"Okay," I tried to say with a little laugh as blood seeped from my ravaged tongue, and spoke a bit louder.

"No," the woman said after about two seconds. "No good, no. No good. Still can't hear you. You're going to have to speak up, miss. We can't hear you."

I took a deep breath and smiled again, boosting my voice to an even higher level.

This time they sat still for a while, about five seconds, before something beside me caught the man's attention.

"Hey, there," he yelled, interrupting me again. "Miss! Miss! Use that thing there, that thing to your right, the bullhorn, the megaphone, right there next to you."

"The microphone?" I asked quizzically. "You want me to use the microphone?"

"Yep, yeah, yeah, that thing right there," the man said as his sidekick nodded.

"Well, I—" I started, because I didn't know what to say. Really, there were a handful of people in attendance, which included myself, all within such proximity that I could reach out and touch any one of them. Without leaning.

"You know," I wanted to say, "I am mishing a tooth, my tongue ish now shliced like a deli ham, and all of you jusht ought to feel lucky that I don't look like Caligula here. *I am bleeding for you people!*"

But I didn't say any of those things. Instead, I picked up the microphone, turned on the PA, and resumed the reading.

And yes, I was aware, I was all too much aware, that when my voice boomed out all over that bookstore as I was reading a column about explaining oral sex to my eighty-five-year-old grandmother and people came from the history section and the gardening section and the biography section to see what all the commotion was about, the last thing they expected was a lisping girl bellowing to a crowd that could have easily fit into a dressing room.

I was almost done reading that piece when two hands raised up from the back row.

"Miss?" the man called out. "Miss? When are you going to get to the part about sexual dysfunction?"

Although I was relieved to learn that he could finally hear me, I stopped, and this time, I sighed.

"What can I do for you, shir?" I said, putting my book down. "We don't talk about shexshual dyshfunction in thish piesh. It'sh about my Nana not undershtanding what Monica did to the preshident under hish deshk. If there had been shexshual dyshfunction at the time of that inshident, Al Gore would now be the leader of thish country."

"No, we mean when are you going to talk about sexual dysfunction in seniors?" the lady said.

"And how to fix it!" the man chimed in. "You wrote the book, you ought to know! Aren't you the doctor that wrote that book?"

I shook my head. "I'm shorry to tell you thish, but you're at the wrong reading," I informed them. "But you know, worse things have happened."

"We're in the wrong place?" the woman said. "Isn't this Barnes and Noble?"

"Yes, but this is Los Angeles," I explained. "I saw seven Barnes and Nobles just on the drive over here."

"Idiot," the woman said as she hit the man.

I just laughed.

The Unseen

M y dog was acting strange. In the kitchen, she barked at thin air, growled at the microwave, and tried to dig her way under the refrigerator.

The cat also got in on the act, hissed and batted at shadows and ran wildly from nothing.

Then, one day, I encountered nothing, too. I was in the dining room when I heard a ruckus erupt in the kitchen, but when I ran to investigate, it was empty, and also eerily quiet.

Something was there. I just didn't know, and couldn't see, what.

After several days of this sort of taunting, I was getting a little freaked out. Fighting the unseen can be a tricky business, as my husband learned the hard way after reading the *Dhammapada* and refusing to kill a blithe little spider that had occupied a parcel of our dining room in between a lampshade and an aromatherapy candle because she "had as much right to a peaceful life as we did, and she was an exceptionally talented web weaver." Sure, it was a pretty web, but the Michelangelo of her species had woven her beautiful home especially so that she could lay about ten thousand eggs in it that would all hatch one day while we were at work, only to be discovered when my husband came home and walked into a solid wall of minute teeny-tiny crawling spiders eager to make his acquaintance. It was not exactly a scene out of *Charlotte's Web*. After he twirled, most likely seizurelike, in the giant wall web, gasping, battling at it and making monkey noises, he realized he was surrounded, and although the infant spiders were practically invisible, he could sense that they were in his hair, under his clothes, and that one crawled near his nostril. He grabbed the vacuum cleaner and in an act of sheer self-defense, massacred them all. He later recalled, "No Navy SEAL could function as well as I did. It was like a horror movie. That was Satan. What was in that web was Satan!"

I tried to tell my husband what was going on now in our kitchen, but this is a man who chooses to exert what little control he has over his own life by ignoring me to the point that one time I actually thought he was dead for several days until I noticed he had fresh crumbs on his shirt.

"Okay, have it your way," I sighed, walking away. "It's probably just a big, hairy, pregnant spider preparing a nest for her endless waves of soon-to-be-born offspring. I'd carry that vacuum cleaner in a holster if I were you, buddy."

Within an hour, our kitchen was completely disassembled and every available surface glowed with a thin, sticky layer of Raid.

"I don't see anything," my husband concluded as a dust bunny the size of a squirrel rested in his hair. "There's nothing here."

Several days later it was his eyes, however, that confirmed the fact that something was indeed horribly wrong in our house.

"Why am I ALWAYS the first one home?" he shouted when I opened the front door. "WHY? Maybe, if just once you were the first one home, YOU could catch another one of nature's aberrations lapping up a cool little drink from the kitchen faucet!"

"Oh my God," I said, feeling the blood drain from my veins. "What did you see? Tell me what you saw!"

"It was a big, dirty, beady-eyed RAT that was hanging around our kitchen sink like it was a rodent saloon," my husband informed me.

"No!" I shrieked in denial. "No! How big was it?"

"A foot, easily a foot," my husband answered. "*Maybe even more.* And then, when it saw me, it leaped from the counter, flew a couple of feet like an action hero toward the microwave, and then vanished. It was like it went to rat school at Cirque du Soleil!"

I gasped. "A Jackie Chan rat??" I cried. "Holy shit. Grab a suitcase. Let's just move. I don't want to live here anymore. We'll just go someplace else, another state where no one knows us. I can't sleep here with a rat. In England, rats wait until people fall asleep and then they bite their noses off. How do I explain that to people? 'Oh, no, heavens no, not a nose job! Plastic surgery? Not me! I'm not that fancy! A *rat* bit it off.' "

"I fought an entire spider colony that looked at me and saw a Hometown Buffet," he asserted. "Those spiders came at me like Costco shoppers descend on the sample ladies with fried foods, and I won. I *won.* I can fight a tiny little rat."

"You said it was a foot long," I replied. "A twelve-inch rat with huge teeth and claws and the legs of Mary Lou Retton is something different than newborn spiders!"

"I FOUGHT SATAN," my husband insisted. "AND SATAN WAS UP MY NOSE."

So reluctantly, and against my better judgment, I said okay, even though I did indeed add that by the way, this is exactly what happens when you won't let me get that maid I've been asking most of my life for, you socialist bleeding heart. Our vacuum cleaner is in no way big enough to suck up a hairy mammal the size of a medium toddler, we're going out to eat every night until you bring me the head of that thing because I know it's pooping out poop pellets of bubonic plague all over my favorite snack foods and I'm having a terrifying vision that if I set foot into that kitchen, that thing will fling itself off the top of the refrigerator and bite me in the neck with its big buck Melissa Gilbert teeth, but fine, if this is what you need to do, fight the rat.

Before fighting the rat, however, there's obviously the shame of having a rat in your house, because it's not like everybody has had one. Popular opinion is that only very dirty people have rats, and even if those certain people who have rats were somewhat dirty, or merely even the smallest bit untidy—and I really mean the smallest bit in the tiniest, most minuscule sense of the word—it would really hurt those people's feelings if that popular senti- ment was directed at them. This is especially the case if these par- ticular people were said to have once had a massive spiderweb in their home, even if it was only because one of them was appreci- ating its Creator's universal right to live, even when it came back to suck the blood out of him.

The Buddhist became a hunter. He left the house headed for Wal-Mart and came home armed with massive spring traps and off-brand peanut butter, on which he wrote with a big black marker, STAY AWAY, LAURIE: RAT BAIT, to make it really official in case our amazing rat could read. He assembled the traps, stuck a glob of peanut butter on them, and we waited.

It didn't take long. Apparently, we had a Mensa rat, because it essentially waited for the hunter to step one foot out of the kitchen before it swung in on its mighty rat trapeze or drove there in its little rodent car, snatched up its peanut butter dinner, and vanished again without consequence.

And it did this again. And again. And again. That rat had moved in, and frankly, it was as unafraid of us as we were ashamed of it.

The Buddhist hunter went to Wal-Mart again and returned with glue traps, placed the peanut butter bait on them, and we waited again.

The first time we checked the traps, there it was, stuck to the very adhesive bottom of the glue panel, and my husband reached for it with a dishtowel.

We couldn't believe what we saw.

"Oh my God," I whispered, covering my mouth.

"Oh Jesus," my husband said. "I mean Buddha."

"Look at it," I said, completely in shock. "Just look at it!"

"I know, I know," he said, shaking his head. "I can't believe it. I don't even know what to say."

"It's so cute!" I cried. "It's so goddamned cute!"

"I guess that's what I was going to say," my husband said, still shaking his head. "It *is* awful cute."

And it was. Our rat was absolutely adorable. Looking up at us with big brown eyes, the barely two-inch, chocolate-colored, velvet-furred "rat" was no menace. Just a tiny little field mouse probably on his way into the big city to find its long-lost family, and maybe even thought we were it.

"Shit," my husband cursed. "It's Stuart Little."

"No, I think it looks more like a girl," I remarked. "In fact, I think she looks like a—"

"DON'T!!" he bellowed. "DON'T NAME IT!!"

"—Molly," I finished.

He just looked at me while Molly looked at us.

I looked at him. I blinked. I looked at him some more.

"No," my husband said sternly. "*We can't keep her.* She's on a glue trap. Do you know what that means? That means she'd have to be on this glue trap forever or we'd have to get her a little mousie wheelchair after her legs got ripped off."

"You're going to kill Molly, aren't you?" I asked, my eyes lowering.

"SHUT UP!!" he said. "How do you think I feel? I have a multitude of conflicting emotions about this! Several months ago I couldn't kill a spider, and now I feel like I should be wearing an

Auschwitz employee badge! This is against everything I believe in. *I may need counseling.* I'll try to take care of Molly as fast and humanely as possible. Or we can OD her on one of your Vicodins and Wal-Mart peanut butter."

"*Those dolls are for special occasions,*" I snapped. "And I just met that rat!"

Before the Buddhist became a murderer, he stopped at the door with Molly on the glue trap in his hands and said simply, "Next time, we're moving."

Let Me In

The temperature on the thermometer outside the back door of my house read 110 degrees.

It felt hotter.

Especially when I went to turn the door handle and I discovered it was locked.

And I was on the wrong side of it.

This was not good. My husband, the only other person in the world who had a key to the house, and who was undoubtedly responsible for locking the door after he came out to say good-bye before he left, was working late and wouldn't be home until well after nightfall. He was working a double shift since a majority of his co-workers were taking vacation days after the news of a Hershey's promotion tore through his department like wildfire. In some parts of the country the lottery isn't the only key to wealth, retiring from your job at Jack in the Box, and finally being able to buy new clothes at Target. There's the lure of promotions as well, and that bug had spread faster at my husband's place of employment than the flu when people use their shirts for tissues. Apparently, "spotters" at randomly selected supermarkets, drugstores, and convenience stores were giving away Jeeps to anyone they saw holding a Hershey's product. Subsequently, the people my husband worked with (minimally comprising college students like himself; the majority consisted of recent recipients of GEDs, role-playing enthusiasts, an entire club of Dungeons & Dragons devotees, select parolees, and a cluster of people who my husband says look "ridden hard and put away wet") had taken to clutching a candy bar during their entire shift.

"So now," my husband told me, "there are a bunch of people running around work with filthy brown hands. They won't *eat* the candy; they just *hold* the candy. Then it melts, and there's chocolate EVERYWHERE. It's as if the M&M characters were beaten with bats in there."

As a result, people started taking vacation time left and right to spend time loitering in Super Wal-Mart with 400 calories and 15 fat grams of pure disappointment clutched in their hot, smudgy hands because since it was a pharmacy and a grocery store combined, they believed it would double their chances.

Now, everybody else knew that NONE of those people was going to win a Jeep—that was a constant in that equation. The thing was, you didn't know who the Hershey Spotter was. I mean, it wasn't like he was dressed up as a big, silver kiss. You didn't spot him, he spotted *you*. And believe me, contest people have learned their lesson from the lottery-winning homeless guy who got seventeen seconds with Katie Couric on the *Today* show, then beat his girlfriend up, was sent to the pokey, and made headlines on CNN. After that, no one's taking the under-the-bridge underdog route anymore. That game has been played and the plebeians are out. It was cute once and it turned into a felony.

Hershey wants soccer games, birthday parties, ballet lessons, not "I'm glad I won this Jeep because now I don't have to take the bus to see my probation officer anymore."

Still, they kept clutching that candy and taking time off. There was, however, one shining moment in this.

"At least," my husband offered, "I now know who washes their hands after a trip to the restroom."

But in my backyard, I was horribly on my own. Well, not exactly.

I had two whining dogs circling my feet, scratching at the door to let them back into the air-conditioning.

Chigger, the old one, impatiently shifted her sea-lion-like body from paw to paw, lest she be mistaken for a corpse and entice the hungry jaws of the younger dog, Bella. She, in turn, was circling the yard, waiting patiently for both Chigger and me to succumb to a heat-induced coma so she could start eating our bodies, and was snacking on her own leg as an appetizer.

It was *so hot.*

No tragedy is complete without the series of mistakes that leads up to it; if only I had let the dogs pee on the floor instead of letting them out; if only I hadn't left the garden hose in a place where Chigger wouldn't have pooped on the drinking end of it; if only I had worn a pair of bike shorts underneath my dress, which would have eliminated profuse sweating, the chafing of my inner thighs, and the painful Chub Rub rash that was now developing.

This wasn't the first time I had been locked out of my house. One sunny morning a year ago, my husband waved to me as I pulled weeds in the front yard, and got in his car after he locked the front door and happily drove away. I was forced to use the phone of my neighbor Marcie, who was home and sadly belting out Melissa Etheridge tunes when I knocked on her door. Her girlfriend had just broken up with her to pursue a life with the Lord and was traveling from state to state on the lesbian gospel circuit, handing out little books entitled *The Only Man You'll Ever Need to Know: Jesus Christ.* Fresh on the rebound, Marcie eagerly showed me all of her tattoos and piercings, even the ones in delicate areas that required some disrobing.

When I finally got my husband on the phone, all I had to say was "Honey, I'm at Marcie's house and she's showing me her body art," and he came right home. Obviously, another trip to Marcie's

House of Rings and Things was out of the question, and, besides, there was no way I could catapult my body over the very high backyard wall, anyway. I thought of dropping Bella over with a note around her collar saying "HELP!!! We're locked out and there's poop on the hose!" but then quickly realized that Bella would take that opportunity to claim her freedom, and if the ship was going down, we were all going to be on it.

The sun had barely begun to set. I sprayed the dogs down with the hose, sat on the back steps with Chigger, and thought about our fate. I imagined my husband coming home to a darkened house, a wide grin spreading across his face as he thought, Got the whole place to MYSELF! Then he'd plop himself down on the couch, dig into a jar of peanut butter for dinner and start surfing the cable channels for Kate Winslet's boobs, which he would undoubtedly find. I, however, would be found about a week later, my body heaped at the back door as my husband said to a detective, "Wow. I just thought she was still at Big Lots."

The detective would say, "Looks like that little mutt made a meal out of her. Went for the tenderloin first," to which my husband would shake his head and reply, "No, that's Chub Rub. Should have worn bike shorts, honey!"

When darkness fell, I started listening for the sound of my husband's car. We had been locked out for hours now, and I was tired, thirsty, and hot. I thought about wringing out my bra for a drink, just to keep me going for the next couple of minutes or until I heard a car pull up. As I was unhooking the back, I heard the phone inside the house ring four times, and then the answering machine pick up.

"Hi, it's me," my husband's voice said. "Another candy clutcher called in. Apparently one of the Civil War reenactors brought his RV down there so they can sleep in the Wal-Mart parking lot and go back in as soon as it opens. It's going to be a long night."

I sat there for a moment, defeated, and I would have cried except that there was no moisture left in my body, and for the first time ever in my life, the thought of chocolate made me furious. I left my bra hooked, and then slowly moved toward the garden hose with my mouth wide open.

Living Urban Legend

"You will never believe what crawled into me at three o'clock in the morning last night," my mother said to me. "I'll give you a hint: It's the last thing you would ever expect!"

"Oh God, Mom," I said, throwing my hands up. "You know, there are some things mothers and daughters should never share. Just because I'm back in therapy doesn't mean I'm now a blank slate on which you now can feel free to inflict a whole other lifetime's worth of damage on. Maybe if you were paying for it, but this time it's on my Visa, so let's pay some attention to that 'boundary' talk we had, all right?"

"Your brain must just be a dustrag, it's so filthy," my mother responded as she looked at me with a cold, blank stare, much like a pigeon's. "No wonder your doctor charges you so much, she has to listen to all of your dirty pervert thoughts. I bet if you cleaned up your act in there, she'd charge you half as much. Now, what I was about to say was this."

I really don't think I would have believed it if I had not seen it for myself. My mother pulled a big, white, folded-up napkin from inside her purse and placed it on the kitchen table.

"THIS," my mother said as she then shook the napkin at me, "CAME FROM MY HEAD! RIGHT IN MY EAR!"

I shook my head. "If you're going to pull out a ball of wax big enough to double as a Glade Solid, count me out! I've pulled things out of myself before that were both frightening and amazing, especially when I have allergies, and sometimes the magnitude of them is so scary I have tried to put them back, but for the benefit for everyone around me I've kept all of that to myself. To *myself*. Let's play the same game here, please."

She gave me the dirty pigeon look and shook the napkin again. "Well," my mom started, "last night I suddenly woke up at three in the morning and heard what sounded like a very loud ocean in my ear. It was so loud, all of this noise! Then I felt something move, and I realized it was in my head."

"My therapist only charges a little bit extra for that," I said as she shot me a look.

She went on to explain that as she was clutching the side of her head and screaming in pain my father told her to go back to sleep, that he was very tired. Insisting that there was something in her ear making noise and moving around, my mom ran into the hallway and stood under the light so my dad could get a better view into her ear.

"It was so loud I kept thinking, Now, I'm a patient person, but even I can't live like this for the rest of my life," she continued, and knowing my mom, she actually probably believed it. "And your father kept saying he couldn't see anything.

"He didn't even bother to put on his right glasses. But who am I to say, you know? There's only what felt like a rat running around in my skull trying to eat my brain like a free wheel of cheese, so, you know, why should he be worried?"

My mother shook the napkin at me again.

"Well, I knew I was dying, I knew I was facing death, and after five minutes, I just thought, All right, all right, God, enough already, where's the friggin' white light?" she went on. "And your father said he couldn't see anything in my ear, and then suddenly, he said he heard a scratching sound."

It was at that point that he suggested very gingerly that they go to the emergency room, which probably wasn't a very good idea on his part. He would have met less resistance had he clubbed her over the head with a dry sausage and then dragged her to the car by her hair, Italian style.

Now, to set the stage, I have to explain a few things. My mother's not a big fan of doctors, although she had no problem dragging her children to them without any warning; one minute I was defending myself against the lobsterlike pinches of my sister in the backseat of the station wagon, and the next, I was in the waiting room, flipping through a year-old issue of Us Weekly, thinking I was about to get an allergy shot from our family doctor, Dr. Goldman. Who just happened to be the father of a boy I went to high school with. A boy I had a tremendous crush on, and who I had, merely two weekends before, danced behind at the Devil House on Teen Night when "What I Like About You" was played, pointing manically and aggressively at the back of his head during the "youuuuuuu" part of the chorus. I didn't particularly mind going to Dr. Goldman's, figuring that as long as I didn't have some sort of skeevy disease or an assortment of open sores, he would see me for the nice, polite, homely girl that I was and pass on a nugget of encouragement to his son, as in "Sure, she's not much to look at, and sure, her overbite looks like a canopy for her chin, but she's a nice girl and you could do a lot worse. By the way, I bet she's a terrific dancer!"

Unfortunately for me, however, I was not at Dr. Goldman's for an allergy shot; I was actually mere moments away from unknowingly about to get my first Pap smear. Unknowingly sitting in the doctor's waiting room, there I was, about to have my romantic teenage hope not simply dashed but severed by a reckless mother who never stopped once to think that a cute Jewish boy just might have enough trouble liking an oily, donkey-toothed Catholic shiksa like me, but bringing home a girl his dad had already seen without her pants on was not exactly fitting into anybody's plan. Had I known I was not getting an allergy shot but was about to live through my own installment of The Vagina Monologues and in addition never again be able to tolerate hearing "What I Like About You" without feeling the hot rush of deep, unforgiving humiliation and uncontrollable rocking back and forth while shaking my head for the duration of the tune twenty-plus years later, maybe I would have been able to say something, run away, or at least fake a seizure. My mother always felt that our medical experiences were on a "need to know" basis, and frankly, she felt that she was the only one who really ever needed to know.

She, however, avoids doctors at all costs, because the last time she went to Dr. Goldman to check out an old-lady vein in her leg, he noticed her conspicuous absence of about a decade and sent her for a complete workup.

And that's when they found cancer in what we like to call her "bra area."

"How can they have *cancer*?" she said as she pointed to her shirt after she got the news. "That's ridiculous! I've never even *used* them!"

The night before her bra area surgery, she motioned to me to follow her up the stairs, and I prepared myself for a tender mother-and-daughter talk and some Terms of Endearment–caliber tears, maybe even sobbing, which could be exciting. I readied myself to be strong, not only for myself but for her, and I took a deep breath before I entered her bedroom. She was sitting on the bed and motioned for me to sit down next to her. She took a deep breath.

Finally, I thought to myself, what I have been waiting almost my whole life to hear: my apology for Dr. Goldman's Pap smear and the love tragedy it cost me. Oh, there were going to be tears, all right.

My mother started. She cleared her throat.

"Listen. If I die under the knife, bury me in the blue beaded gown with these earrings and the matching shoes. My Death Outfit is together right here in this bag. This was my runner-up outfit to wear to your wedding in case I lost a little weight with all of the aggravation you caused me insisting that you had to have a WOMAN marry you, but I never lost an ounce, although I'll bet you every gift you got that you aren't married after all and that woman was just after a free meal, a couple of beers, and some dancing. Which she got—did you see how much cheese she ate? I did. I was watching. I saw. I bet it was her first week on Atkins, I do. It doesn't matter that I'm still too fat to wear this gown, I'll be dead and laying down, so just don't zip up the back and it will look fine, and most of my bulk is air, anyway.

"Now, when you bring all of the relatives back to the house after my funeral, you'd better serve Boar's Head cold cuts. If you get the cheap meat and serve that to people who have just cried over my limp, lifeless body, I swear to God I will come back and haunt the living shit out of you. And if you feel like being a funny ass and burying me without panties, I'm not coming back alone. I'll bring some dead clowns with me."

"You sure can put the 'fun' in funeral, Mom," I replied.

The next day, when my mom checked into the hospital, the nurse pointed to the garment bag and said, "What's this? Our dinners aren't that formal. Most patients don't even wear pants."

"Well, after you people kill me," my mother responded, "I figured I ought to look a little nice in case I meet someone I know in the morgue after you suck the blood out of my veins and replace it with antifreeze. And make sure you suck all the air out, and I mean all. Jump on me if you have to. There's a dress I have to fit into."

I never got my apology, and my mother beat cancer like it was a prepubescent daughter with a fresh mouth, but with this story about the roar in my mother's ear I was finally getting some satisfaction from the fact that for the first time in a long time my mother had been dragged to the doctor against her will.

Apparently, the roaring in my mother's ear was getting louder, almost unbearable, and after some coaching and the promise that she could buy anything she saw on QVC the next day, my dad finally got her to the hospital, checked her into the emergency room, and then waited for someone to help them.

And I'm using the word "help" as a general term here.

Perhaps she was just making compelling medical conversation, perhaps she was just passing on odd and chilling trivia relating to people who have a feeling they have multilegged creatures taking a stroll in an orifice, but as the nurse was pouring alcohol into my mother's ear, the idiot mentioned that it was quite common for insects, particularly roaches, to crawl into people's body cavities while they slept.

Now, I firmly believe that it should be against the law for any medical professional to say that to anyone, let alone a woman who would put a house up for sale and move to an entirely different zip code if she so much as spotted a boll weevil husk in a cabinet. Suggesting that my mother might have had a roach crawling around in her house, *let alone in her head,* was equivalent to saying that she went to church six times a week for the free wafers and wine.

"Stop right there," my mother immediately said to the nurse, and then called out to my father. "It's time to bring in the Death Outfit Bag. This one says it could be a roach, and if that's a roach walking around in my brain, I command you to shoot me dead. I mean it, *I want to die.* I can't live a moment longer knowing there was a dirty, vermin-covered, shit-eating roach in my body. My house is not filthy, I will have you know, my house is NOT FILTHY! I clean, and I also have a girl who comes every other week! She breaks things and doesn't understand English, but that is the price I am willing to pay for a clean house! She vacuumed Styrofoam peanuts and blew the whole thing up, but that's how far I am willing to go to make my home roach-free!"

My dad tried to calm her down as the doctor took over for the big-mouthed nurse and came at my mother's head with a very long pair of tweezers. According to my mother, the whole emergency room became very quiet as the doctor went fishing in her ear and began pulling the invader out, bit by bit.

In the first search mission, he found a leg; the second time in, he brought up a body section; and then, finally, on the third attempt, he was rewarded with a wing. A *wing*. In the emergency room, a cheer burst into the air, largely due to my father.

"It's a wasp!" he exclaimed as my mother broke down into tears of joy. "It's a *wasp*!"

"Wow, Mom," I said as she unfolded the napkin, "you're a living urban legend! I bet if you went home and forwarded a bunch of Microsoft e-mail to test their new tracking system, Bill Gates really *would* pay you five dollars a pop!"

"Look," she said, holding up the napkin with pieces of the wasp scattered on it. "If you put him back together again, it's over an inch long! Wasps are very attracted to nice-smelling things, so it all makes sense. I had just gotten my new Joan Rivers Now and Forever Fragrance Set from QVC that day and it must have been just a magnet to that wasp."

"I can't wait to tell everyone that a wasp tried to nest in my mom's head!!" I yelled. "God! This is so exciting!"

"If you think that's exciting," my mom said with a smile, "I just bought a case of earplugs from QVC! I'm never going to so much as close my eyes without plugging my ears up like a leaky ship."

I nodded and laughed, daring to remind her that unless she slept with a snorkel attached, her open, snoring mouth was just another unexplored, mysterious cave to the unholy.

An Open Letter to Todd at Cox Cable

Dear Todd:

First off, I want to say that I'm sorry for yesterday. I didn't mean it. I really didn't. I was on hold for seven minutes when you finally answered, and to tell you the truth, I just never expected it. Who would? When you clicked on the line and the first thing you said was "It's a great day at Cox Cable! This is Todd, how may I assist you?" I didn't laugh at you on purpose. I never meant for you to take it personally. It's just a knee-jerk reaction, like when you see someone trip over a step, or when the wind blows someone's skirt up. You know, life's little bonuses, a golden nugget from God's Comedy Store. You just point and laugh heartily, because that's the silver lining of someone else's misfortune.

And I really wasn't poking fun at you when I asked if you got a raise, saw some action last night, or discovered via a hand mirror that the Rogaine is starting to work. I really wanted to know what makes a great day at Cox Cable. Is there a list of criteria that must happen before the day receives the title of "great"? I mean, what distinguishes "a great day at Cox Cable" from "a day at Cox Cable"? Like I said, maybe there's something good to eat in the cafeteria, or no one brought a gun to work, or someone complimented you on your jaunty hat. See, Todd, you just can't toss "It's a great day at Cox Cable" out there and not expect us to develop a curiosity. That's human nature, man! We want to know!

I noticed you became withdrawn from the conversation at that point, and I knew that somehow I had hurt you. You were so distant, so formal, so . . . cold. There, I've said it! You were cold, Todd, *cold!* I could hear it in your voice, the sudden chill, and I felt you backing away from me. And then, in an instant, you were gone. I had lost you. Maybe forever.

In fact, you wouldn't even answer me when I asked you if taking IFC off of basic cable was an evil ploy to get people to buy into digital, or if there really is a truck equipped with special radar that drives through neighborhoods to catch people stealing cable TV. And what happened to the lady on the commercial who was caught? Was she found guilty? Did she go to prison? Did she get the death penalty? Is she being tortured to give up names of other cable thieves? Was she the kingpin of the whole operation?

But Todd, you said nothing. It was clearly over between us. You wanted to push me away, get some distance, forget that I was ever a part of your life. You did that, Todd, you did that. So I ask you, is it still a great day at Cox Cable, Todd? IS IT? Because I have to tell you, the sun isn't so shiny over here. It's not a great day at my house, Todd, because there's something else that you need to know, but you didn't want to hear it. No, no, you just brushed me away, but I'm going to say it anyway, before God and everybody RIGHT NOW: I want HBO with my digital cable, Todd!

I want HBO!!

Until next time,

Laurie

I'm Gonna Kick
Your Ass

It was not the firm, shiny loop that initially caught my attention. It was not.

It was the long, sinewy, arms, thin and stringy and so pale they were nearly light green, lifting up the twenty-pound bag of Sensitive Stomach dog food from the counter into the cart. As he lifted the bag, the owner of those arms grunted—no, no, no, forgive me, "grunted" is too strong a word, too gracious a word, too complimentary; mewled or whimpered is actually more accurate, much more precise a description—causing me to wonder what kind of nancy was wrestling with the bag, since I was the one who placed it on the counter to begin with and I can barely lift a jug of water with two hands.

And that is when, that is precisely when, I turned and saw it.

The Flippy Hair.

Flippy hair that was so extraordinarily flippy that any girl in the graduating class of 1978 would have eagerly traded her Sun-In Sassoon Gunne Sax Pearl White Tooth Drops soul for just a portion of the flip. Just a portion of it. It had kick, it had zing, it had pizzazz, it had chutzpah. The flip was absolutely amazing, it turned upward, away from the face, Farrah Fawcett–style, in an almost full 360-degree loop all the way around the head like a halo. It looked like the creator had taken a bowl, a can of Aqua Net, and a wind tunnel and just went nuts. In the age of Chrissy, Jack, Janet, and nights spent sipping tequila sunrises at the Regal Beagle, it would have been the perfect hair, with the exception of one detail: It was on a guy.

It was on the guy with the linguine arms. And it looked stupid.

Now, I will admit that I unabashedly stared, although I did not know this at the time. I only surmised it later, when I realized I could not have absorbed all the detail of his complicated coiffure had I not taken in such a deep, long, thirsty look. *What is going on with that?* was my first thought. Still wrestling with the dog food bag as if it were a sixty-pound swordfish, the Flippy Hair Guy whimpered again, dropped the bag into the cart like it was a bag of cement, and walked away, his macaroni arms whipping in the air like fleshy shoelaces.

I turned to the cashier and tried to meet her gaze, but she was busy scanning my other items. When she finally looked at me, I stood there, trying to detect a common sense of puzzlement in her eyes concerning the Flippy Hair Guy, but there was none, only the pure boredom that you can only find in the soulless gaze of a teenager working retail. Mummies have been found in both China and Mexico that have had more complex expressions on their faces than the empty facial canvas of the minimum-wage employee in the middle of a shift.

I didn't say anything to the cashier until she handed me my receipt and a pen and I started to sign it.

"Sure is some hairstyle on that guy," I said with a smile, trying to prompt or lure her into a Flippy Hair discussion. "Sure was all flippy. Like a fancy lampshade."

"Mmmmmm," the cashier said as she leaned up against the counter and stared off into the distance and chewed on the tip of a pen.

Hmmmph, I thought as she gave me nothing, *nothing*. I took my stuff and left.

I thought about the Flippy Hair Guy all the way to the car. I mean, I just didn't get it. Why was his hair all flipped and curled up like that? It was like *lady hair*. Crazy lady hair. Why? What would possess someone to invest all of that time and energy in something so complex, so intricate, and yet so useless? I had never seen anyone with hair like that, ever. It was ridiculously bad. So bad that that guy really did look like an idiot, you know. He really did. I thought, what kind of a person walks around with hair like that? What an idiot, I thought again. What an idiot.

And then I stopped.

And I listened to that voice that was doing the thinking, and although it sounded very, very familiar—*very, very* familiar—it did not sound *exactly* like mine. It sounded a little bit different.

Hit with a metaphorical bolt of lightning, I understood.

"Oh my God," I hissed as I ran to the car, pushing the cart. "Oh my God!!"

When I got to my parking space, I threw the dog food into the backseat, threw myself into the front, and said calmly, "Mom, get out of my head."

"What?" my mother's voice said. "You know what that crazy kid looked like? He looked like he was wearing a big hair doughnut is what."

"Get out peacefully, Ma," I said, trying to stay calm. "Please don't make me hit myself in the head while I'm sitting here alone in the car in a crowded parking lot. Because I'll hit you out if I have to, I will. I will. "

"His poor, poor mother," my mother's voice continued. "I hope she lives very far away and doesn't have to look at him and be embarrassed in front of her friends the way I was every time you would come home with a new hair thing. Remember the black, stringy Wicked Witch of the West hair you had? I do. You made kids at Kmart cry with that hair, they were so scared. You pretended to cast a spell on them as they were running away! Remember the bleached-bang thing you had hanging in front of your face? Huh? Huh? You got into three car accidents that year, just because the 'seagull' look was in. And then, the worst! That Raggedy Ann hair. It was like hair yarn! All of those knots! Would a brush have killed you? It almost killed me!"

"It wasn't Wicked Witch of the West hair. I was a death rocker. I had dull, clumpy long black hair and it kicked ass," I explained calmy to the ignorant voice. "And I wasn't trying to be a seagull, I was a pioneer in the world of New Wave, and that wasn't Raggedy Ann hair, I had dreadlocks before people started buying fake ones and getting them glued to their heads. Mine took time, effort, and a gallon of Herbal Essences Conditioner, on seven consecutive nights before my wedding, to take out. The resulting hairball was as big as a brain, but my dreads rocked."

"Your hair didn't rock," the voice said. "You looked like an idiot. A big, stupid idiot with nothing to prove."

"Get out or I'm going to start saying the F-word, Ma," I promised.

"Whatever," the voice said. "It's weird in here, anyway. Just how many drugs did you do? It's like a graveyard with all of these dead brain cells floating around. They're like little beetle shells! It smells just like your old room in here, and there's a cup with old Pepsi all dried up and crystallized on the bottom. Disgusting. That's my cup. I want it back, and I want it back *clean*. You know, I just saw what you and your therapist said about me. Tell her she's an idiot just like you! Hey, pay me a hundred and fifty bucks an hour and I'll talk shit about me, too!"

"Fu—" I started.

"Save your filthy breath, I'm out!" the voice said, and with a *poof!* she was gone.

My hair was not idiotic, I reassured myself. I did *not* look like an idiot. My hair was cool. I *always* had cool hair. Just because my mom didn't get it, just because she's old and out of the loop, she thinks that just because she didn't understand my hair, because she wasn't of my generation, that it was automatically *stupid*. Well, that's my mom for you. *That's my mom, no reservations about broadcasting her opinions anywhere to anybody.*

Oh God.

And then I gasped, remembered vocalizing my own comments to the cashier about Flippy Hair Guy, and my hand flew up to my mouth.

Sure was some flippy hair on that guy.

That's *some* hairstyle. Like a fancy lampshade.

I understood at that moment that I had just crossed a threshold. Within a moment, and without even realizing what I had done, I had taken a dreadful leap over the grim gorge of a generational divide and was now standing on the old, nearly dead side of life, all because of Stupid Flippy Hair Guy.

Youth was at least a canyon's length away, taunting me with echoes of my hair past. The day had finally come when I didn't understand hair, and that could mean only one thing: I was out of the loop. I was not now, and could never again be, cool.

Honestly, what was next for me? If I didn't understand Flippy Hair Guy's deal, what was waiting just around the corner for me? Pantyhose with sandals? Wearing spandex over an ass the size of a futon that had the movement of yogurt? Hometown Buffet at four P.M. to catch the early-bird special?

Stupid Flippy Hair Guy, I thought as tears of anger, sadness, and certainly a tinge of melodrama—just in case I was going to recount this story later to anyone—blossomed in my eyes. Stupid Flippy Hair Guy. What I did not understand fifteen minutes ago began to change quickly, and without mercy became something akin to loathing.

Was he really stupid, or was Stupid Flippy Hair Guy so cool that I simply didn't get it?

I was furious at Flippy Hair Guy. Why did he go and have to do that? Go and make me old with his stupid hair! AND HE WASN'T EVEN COOL. MAYBE. He worked at a pet food store. In my day, cool guys didn't work at pet food stores, they worked at record stores or just didn't work at all (fill in your own blanks there). And they certainly didn't have spaghetti arms that couldn't even lift a bag of dog food, arms that were covered in freckles the size and color of cornflakes, CORNFLAKES! I could have bit his arm right off, probably pinched them off, they looked like they were squeezed out from a Play-Doh machine. That's how googley they were, like they were boneless. Flippy Hair Guy was basically a Muppet with no fur. Pretty much that's what he was. And he whimpered. I heard him whimper.

That is not cool. Whimpering is never cool.

I mean, clearly, I cried to myself as I drove home, this is a guy who not only owns a curling iron BUT WORKS IT WITH A DEGREE OF MAGNIFICENT SKILL, and, unlike myself, was not only gifted with it, but ambidextrous as well. I didn't see one single neck or forehead burn. He used it much like the wand of a wizard, and with one wave of it, he had made me into my mother.

The bastard.

I really wanted to tell someone, but I couldn't admit that I had passed on to the other side. I was scared. I was horrified. I was ashamed.

As well as apparently obsessed. I had found myself entirely obsessed with the cornflake-freckled, Play-Doh-limbed Muppet known as Stupid Flippy Hair Guy. I thought about him all the time, wondering, *just wondering, what did that hair mean?* I turned through pages of magazines, searching for a similar hairstyle, for some point of reference. When I watched TV, I looked for anything resembling his tube of curl. I found myself contemplating whether Joan Rivers would give him a glowing or negative review, or whether the *Queer Eye* crew would take my side or his. I needed something, I needed anything. Not only to be able to identify him, it was absolutely essential in being able to identify ME.

The next day at the pet food store, after I walked up and down each aisle numerous times, the Stupid Flippy Hair Guy was nowhere to be found, and I was sure he was sitting around somewhere underneath a massive helmet hair dryer with Styrofoam cups as curlers, getting ready for his next big day out in public. I decided, however, to turn his absence into my advantage.

After I hauled the bag of dog food purposefully onto the counter of a cashier I had never openly expressed my grandma attitude to, I decided to test her vulernability to subtle interrogation.

"Pretty earrings," I said to her.

"Thank you," she said as she shook her head to activate the auditory element of her jewelry, thus exposing herself as an easy, malleable target. "I just have a thing for feathers. And little bells."

"It's a good look—and sound—on you," I nodded. "Speaking of looks, where's the guy with the . . . hair?"

She looked puzzled. "Which guy?"

"You know," I said with a wave of my hand. "That one guy who looks like he spends his nights sleeping in a wind tunnel with his hair rolled up around hot dogs. The one who looks determined to outflip Valerie Bertinelli's hair, as if they were in a duel."

"Oh, him," she said. "I haven't seen him today. He must be off."

"Is his hair is always like that?" I asked. "Or did I see him on a day when perhaps he was auditioning to play 'Julie McCoy' in a school production of *Love Boat*?"

"Yeah, it's pretty much always been like that since I worked here," the cashier replied.

"Do you know why?" I asked

She shook her head.

"Well, I'm sure people comment on it all the time," I continued, to which she shook her head again.

"No," she replied. "You're the only person who's ever said anything about it to me."

I was flabbergasted. It was worse than I had thought, because, apparently, other people found the Flippy Hair perfectly acceptable, or were perhaps so intimidated by it they were afraid to tackle the problem verbally.

But that Friday, as Spaghetti Arms wrestled the Sensitive Stomach dog food bag like it was an angry bear fighting a park ranger for a two-day-old pre-eaten corncob, I looked *carefully* this time, and almost had to stop myself from reaching out and touching the hair, like it was a burner glowing on a stove.

And just like a burner, I felt my face get hot. No matter how hard I studied that flip, I was just not *getting* that hair. It was impossible. The hair and I were not communicating, we had reached an impasse. I did not understand.

That hair had made me obsessed.

That hair had made me confused, it had made me doubt myself.

That hair had made me cross the generational divide.

That hair had made me old.

That hair had made me mad.

I hated that hair so bad I wanted to *fight* it.

"I'm gonna kick your hair's ass," I whispered to the Flippy Hair under my breath, even though my bag of dog food had done a pretty damn good job of it already, as several purply bruises had floated to the surface of the cornflake skin, as if kidneys had suddenly bobbed up in a bowl of cereal.

"I just hate you," I continued under my breath, and then added for dramatic effect, and to no one's astonishment but my own, "I hate your hair! Kidney arms!"

When my husband asked me that weekend why our kitchen was suddenly stocked with a year's supply of Sensitive Stomach pellets in twenty-pound bags, I was naturally reluctant and somewhat embarrassed to explain.

"There was a sale," I lied.

"I don't believe that for one minute, Miss Uncontrollable Id," my husband replied immediately. "If there were twenty boxes of expensive shoes in this kitchen, twenty boxes of books you were never going to read, or twenty bags of Double Stuff Oreos, I'd give that answer the green light. Or if you were a fat little red dog with a farting problem, maybe. But an item that serves another being's needs aside from your own? Not a chance. Spill that empty soul of yours, sister."

I sighed.

"There's this guy at the pet food store . . ." I started.

"Ah-HA!" my husband yelled. "And you have a crush on him! You think he's cute! Did he lift the bag of dog food with his pinky to impress you?"

"Hardly," I replied. "I think he popped six vertebrae and punctured a lung just by trying to *slide* it off the counter. His bones are like crazy straws, you can almost see the blood being sucked through. And I hate him. I don't just hate him, I *haaaaaaate* him."

"What did he do?" my husband asked.

I stood directly in front of my husband and put my hands on my hips. "He curls his hair!" I bellowed. "Stupid Flippy Hair Guy *curls his hair*. And he thinks it's cool."

"So because a drag queen works at the pet food store we can no longer walk in our kitchen," my husband said. "These are bigger than sandbags, Laurie. It looks like we're getting ready to battle the Galveston Flood."

"He's not a drag queen," I cried. "He has eyebrows. How simple it would be if this problem just boiled down to a muted cross-gender sexual identity! You don't understand. I don't *get* his hair. I think he looks like an idiot."

"Um, if you don't immediately identify yourself as Laurie Notaro and not Laurie Notaro's mom, I'm going to take a hammer to my head," my husband said.

"And that's exactly why I hate him," I confessed. "The next thing you know, I'll be going to church six times a week, shoving Afrin up my nose every five seconds, yelling at homeless people to get jobs, and carrying my blood-pressure machine with me in my purse. I can't be my mom, not yet. I'm not ready, but Stupid Flippy Hair Guy is forcing the hands of time!"

My husband took a deep breath. "Maybe it's time you reentered the workforce," he said with a strained look. "Maybe all of this time by yourself isn't very healthy for you. Are you spending more time than normal talking into the mirror?"

"So that's what you think?" I shrieked back. "Well, wait till you see him if you think I'm so stir-crazy and insane! He has cornflake skin!"

And then I had a wonderful idea.

"That's it!" I cried. "You have to come with me. You have to come to the pet food store so you can be the control group! That's how I'll know if it's me or if it's . . . him. *Because, I tell you, this is getting serious. SERIOUS. I am going to kick his hair's ass.*"

"I am not going to the pet food store to gawk at some dork's hair," my husband said defiantly. "And you can't make me."

An hour later, from a terrific spying perch, I spied a purply, blotchy bruised arm trying to scoop up a bala shark in a tiny net.

"That's him!" I whispered excitedly to my husband. "Those are the bruises from the same bag of dog food you fell on!"

My husband gasped. "It's like he has Cling Wrap for skin," he said sadly. "I can see right through him. He has arms like ET!"

"I know," I said with a slow nod. "See what I mean?"

Then, all of a sudden, the Flippy Hair Guy stepped back, directly into our field of vision.

"You are an idiot," he said staunchly. "Three hundred pounds of dog food for THAT? Are you out of your mind? I can't even believe I let you talk me into coming down here for that! His hair is FINE!"

I didn't know what to say, I was completely stunned.

"That's because," I stuttered. "That's because . . . he cut it. He cut the Flippy Hair! It's gone! The Flippy Hair is gone! It just looks like normal hair!"

It was true. Every lock of flippiness had been severed and discarded like skin from a peeling sunburn. What remained was a regular haircut, short all the way around, so short we could even see his transparent, crazy, straw cauliflower ears.

"Why do you think he would do that?" I asked.

"I don't know, Laurie," my husband said, looking straight at me. "Maybe he heard someone call his hair a 'fancy lampshade.' Maybe he heard someone say he had 'crazy-lady hair.' Maybe he found out that someone wanted to kick his hair's ass."

"I would have done something about the freckles first," I said quietly. "They're alarming."

"SHUT UP," my husband said. "Just shut up. And if you see anyone else with weird hair from now on, just pretend it's a wig, all right?"

"It's just like Samson," I said, shaking my head as we walked out of the store. "All of his power and intrigue is gone, vanished, dried up. Just like that. He's just an average pet store guy now."

"I thought you would be happy," my husband said, completely and entirely out of patience.

Truth is, I thought I would be happy, too. But as I turned and looked one last time down the aquarium aisle as the No More Flippy Hair Guy stuck his so-pale-they-were-almost-green noodly arms into another fish tank, I just felt sad.

I Ruined Everything

Just as my husband and I were sitting down to dinner, the phone rang.

My jaw tightened in the full clench of aggravation. This happens in the moments before my husband announces, "I'm not here," which also just happens to coincide with every single time the phone rings or the doorbell shrieks. It's a proclamation that he regards as complete absolution from answering either, as if his last name was Bush, he was eighteen, and there was a draft going on.

"Why can't we just screen?" he repeatedly asks after he's declared his motto and I throw him a dirty look before I am forced to get up and do the dirty work myself.

"Because I have an eighty-six-year-old grandmother who may need our help and is not technologically advanced enough to leave a message communicating that she is in danger!" I yelled. "You've heard them! Her messages are composed of a million 'Hello?'s, mixed in with a dozen 'Laurie, can you hear me?'s, then topped off with her unsuccessful attempt to hang up the phone, followed by an hour or so of the audio of JAG or whatever Lifetime movie she's watching. Trying to decipher her messages is like collecting random sounds from space. Even when you put all of the pieces of the puzzle together, it then just becomes a riddle."

"Well, I'm fine with screening," my husband said. "It's the least technology can do for me. If Safeway keeps track of everything I buy, if I get so much porn junk e-mail that even a thirteen-year-old boy would get sick of it, if Pottery Barn can sell my name and address to every catalogue ever mailed, including the one for a new Vietnamese wife who would be happy to pick up the phone, then technology can do me this one favor. I can screen. I'm fine with screening."

"Clearly you're at one with screening," I protested. "Clearly. The issue is not how clear you are. The issue is how cloudy you see the big picture."

"I don't know why you bought a pig picture," he said, barely listening to me. "But I'm sure it looks great."

I have been through several attempts at psychological warfare to remedy this situation: I told my husband that if he wasn't going to answer the phone, he wasn't allowed to give out our number, but everyone he knew already had it; when someone called for him and he repeatedly mouthed the words "I'm not here!" in front of me, I'd tell the caller, "He says to tell you he's not here," but that didn't work because all of his friends figure he doesn't call me The Mean Lady for nothing

So with my jaw clenched so tight I swore I heard teeth crack— which is not as difficult as it may sound when your teeth are as sturdy as Bubble Wrap—I looked at the phone tiredly, really only wanting to eat my dinner in peace, when all of a sudden, a hand reached over and picked up the phone.

"Hello?" my husband said into the receiver.

I gasped in amazement. I couldn't believe what I was seeing or hearing.

After all, he had *picked up the phone.* The universe had just basically opened up with an infinite number of possibilities. A miracle had happened. Who knew what else was in store for us, I thought to myself, then suddenly had an overwhelming urge to run outside and see if an image of the Virgin Mary was now projected on the side of my house.

"Yes, yes, this is he," my husband said into the receiver. "Really? Oh, well—um, sure. Okay."

And then he vanished into his office for a good twenty minutes. I ate dinner alone, but believe me, it was a small price to pay for having half the phone responsibility lifted from my wrists.

A couple of nights later we were again halfway through dinner when the phone rang. My husband actually got up and answered it, then, once again, retreated into his office. Twenty minutes later, he finally came out. He said nothing.

Now, naturally, it was killing me not to know who was calling. Why all of a sudden was he willing and able to answer the phone? Did he have a secret lady friend? Was he a sleeper agent like Chuck Barris? Had he picked up some side work in the phone-sex trade but was too embarrassed to tell me? He certainly was being sneaky about it, and the third time the phone rang and he answered it, I demanded an explanation.

"What is going on?" I bellowed as soon as he emerged from his office after another twenty-minute chat. "Who are you talking to? I am onto you! Are you taking a hit out on me? Because I'm onto you! Are you cheating? Because I'm onto you! If you're buying another wife, I'll tell you right now, I am not sharing closet space and she's going to have to keep her little pigs outside!"

"Don't be ridiculous!" he said as he laughed at me. "It was some political-opinion poll. They just wanted to ask me questions, and now they call all the time. I guess they like me."

"Oh," I said, startled that I had been so off base. The thought of pesky opinion pollsters/questionnaire people had never crossed my mind. And of course, my husband being the nicer half of our union, he was far too polite to tell them to knock it off and would painfully endure a twenty-minute Q&A session.

So I did, the next time they called and my husband wasn't home.

"Please take us off your list," I said firmly to the pesky pollster.

"Are you sure?" he had the nerve to ask.

"Am I sure?" I replied, imagining a neoconservative minion on the other end of the phone. "Well, let me put it this way: I'm as sure as I am that I'm going to SUE YOU FOR HARASSMENT if you ever call here again! You people have been bothering my poor husband over and over again, and he's just too nice to tell you to buzz off! He's lucky that he has a wife like me who will tell little pests like you what you can do with your dumb old questions! Ever hear of the 'Do Not Call' list? Well, shrimp, you're ON IT! Wait—I'M on it! No—are you on it? Or is it me? I don't know. Just remember the 'Do Not Call' part! Don't call him anymore!"

"He sure sounds lucky to me," the pollster said. "Fine, we'll take you off."

"That's what I thought you'd say," I said slyly and hung up. I smiled. I was thrilled. I had saved my husband. A wife's duty done.

And when he finally came home, I couldn't wait to tell him that I had released him from poll duty, opened up the cage, and let him fly right out.

"You're free!" I added. "They'll never call here again!"

Instead of jumping for joy that I had severed his shackles, his mouth dropped and he just stared at me, probably in amazement, I thought.

"They're never going to call here again?" he asked slowly.

"Never!" I said excitedly, trying to convey the good deed that I had done.

"Now, why," he said as he continued looking at me without even cracking a joyous grin, "would you do that?"

I was stunned. "Aren't you happy? Aren't you happy that I got them to stop calling?" I asked.

"Why would I be happy?" he replied. "Because someone finally asked for my opinion?"

"But—" I tried to interject.

"But nothing!" my husband almost yelled. "Oh my God. Didn't you ever wonder when you see a poll on CNN or in the newspaper who those poll people are? It was me! It *was me!* I was a poll person! They had finally found me after all these years. Someone finally wanted to know what I thought. And now you ruined the whole thing!"

"I ruined everything?" I asked. "I didn't mean to."

"*Do you know who I am?*" my husband said, and then suddenly pointed to himself. "I am 'undecided.' You know how you see the 'undecided' vote on polls? Well, when I felt like it, when the mood struck, that was me! I was the Undecided Guy!!"

"I'm really sorry," I said shamefully. "I had no idea you led a secret life as the Undecided Guy."

"Well, I *did*," my husband said. "Are you sure they're never going to call back?"

"Pretty sure," I said as I nodded slowly. "I called him a 'shrimp' and threatened legal action."

"The Undecided Guy is dead," my husband said as he shook his head sadly and sat down on the couch. "He barely had a chance to live."

Then the phone rang, and even before I had a chance to offer to get it, my husband lifted up his hand, looked at me, and said simply, "I'm not here."

"You know what?" I said, looking straight at him. "Then neither am I."

Attack of the XL Girl

A s soon as I opened the door to the boutique and took a quick look around, I shook my head, sighed, and went on in. It had been this way all day.

Every stop my friend Meg and I made was like another flash of bad skinny-girl déjà vu. I'd open the door, take two steps in, and there we were, confronted by racks filled with nothing but really cool funky designer clothes.

Initially, I was in heaven. I was visiting Meg in Seattle shortly after she had her baby, Carmen, and I was more than excited about my shopping opportunities. In my hometown, pickings are slim, and unless I wake up each day with the desire to dress "drone" and head to my local Gap, Banana Republic, or J. Crew like everyone else, I'm a little more than slightly out of luck. Since Meg, being a new mother with an infant, had been basically confined to the house for eight weeks, she was itching to get out. "I want to go shopping. I'm dying to buy something without an elastic panel that stretches from my crotch to my waistband," she said to me over the phone a couple of days before I arrived. "I don't even care that I'm completely fat right now, I am just dying for some real clothes!"

Secretly, I was a little delighted because Meg had always been my rail-thin friend who made me look like a Pittsburgh Steeler when I stood next to her. She could eat troughs of any given dairy product without consequence and once actually wrinkled her nose at a box of Godiva, explaining chirpily, "You know, I'm just not a chocolate kind of person."

Although Meg lacked the very qualities that I counted as some of my finest and I somewhat doubted that her DNA was indeed human, she had remained a wonderful friend for over a decade, and now, for once, I was going to see her fat!

After my plane landed, I met Meg at the curb, where she picked me up in her Bronco, which was now outfitted with a baby seat. As she jumped out of the front seat and ran to open the tailgate, I stood back and screeched.

"Liar! Liar!" I yelled as I pointed at Meg and her "I had a baby basically yesterday but am going to the Oscars tonight in a dress made from Cling Wrap" figure. "Who are you, Sarah Jessica Parker? Come on, you said you were FAT, and I gorged on pretzels and Pepsi the whole way down here thinking that for once our butts were going to be in the same BMI category! This is so not fair! If you don't show me a stretch mark right now, I'm grabbing a bag of Hershey's Kisses and a six-pack and I'm getting back on that plane!"

"I can do better than a stretch mark," Meg said as she laughed at me. "I had a nine-pound baby and got forty-four stitches as a reward!"

"Ewwww," I said with a gasp. "That's what you get for being Miss Healthy! See, this is where a slothlike lifestyle packed with sugar, processed foods, and caffeine would have really paid off for you and given you a baby with a small little softball head!"

"Oh my God, look at how fat I am!" Meg cried, outstretching her arms. "I now have two fat rolls!"

"Oh, Meg," I said, putting my arms around her. "Poor, sweet, skinny Meg. Those aren't fat rolls, my friend; those are your boobies."

So not only was Meg still Depression-era thin, she now had

cleavage to boot, which up until then had been the one and only area between the two of us where I reigned supreme, even if I had it on my back, too.

As if the fact that Meg was now buxom weren't enough to drive me mad, once we went shopping the next day, things quickly began falling apart more quickly than a Twinkie dipped in hot chocolate. There, in front of me, were rows and rows of the kind of clothes I struggle to find, all laid out before me simply for the taking. Overwhelmed by excitement and the possible damage these incredible finds were going to have on my Visa bill next month, I made fashion sparks fly from my fingertips as I flipped through the items on the rack like they were a deck of cards. Again and again, I caught my breath and gasped, "Oh!" with desire to a brown velvet waistcoat with antique jet buttons—but it was a size six. Not gonna work with my 38C torpedoes unless the whole thing was made out of very forgiving spandex and a Seal-a-Meal machine. "Oh!" to a striped pair of corduroy bell-bottoms à la Janis Joplin in her heyday (which I guess translates to "alive"), but alas, that size four wasn't going to fit unless I was able to clone the original pair and sew the two of them together. "Oh!" to the most darling fifties-style aqua poplin day dress, but then the size-two tag squashed my hopes like a potato bug beneath the sole of a strappy, three-inch, skinny-heeled sandal. Not compatible with this user, unless the dress came with a hidden expansion panel the size of a movie screen.

This happened again and again and again. Size six. Size four. Two. Zero. And then, when I saw that a slovenly size-eight skirt on the clearance rack was the fat lady in this circus, I knew I was in the wrong freak show.

I was in a Skinny Store, where double-digit girls were not allowed, mainly because in this single-digit world, they plainly didn't exist.

I was dully reminded of an experience several months previous when I wandered through SoHo during a short trip to New York City. I had decided that during my trip, I would allow myself one extravagance, and I had decided I was going to buy a dress—maybe even a "not on sale" dress—in the one of the funnest parts of the coolest city in the world. That was going to be my gift to my-self. A great, wonderful, expensive dress. I was dying to throw my money away, I was dying to simply give someone my money, I tell you, but alas, no one would take it. Nanette Lepore didn't want it, and neither did Anna Sui or Cynthia Rowley. I might as well have been on a scavenger hunt with no clues, because that's the kind of luck I was having trying to find a size L dress in New York City. Fat money was apparently no good there. Salespeople looked at me as if I were a mythical beast, something only whispered about in the safety of a shadowy stockroom. Even size eights didn't belong in this world, because the only clothes displayed were the zeroes, twos, fours, and sixes. I felt like the biggest girl in the universe—as if I had been exposed to Chernobyl-like amounts of radiation and had just flattened entire Japanese villages simply with the crumbs that had fallen from my mouth.

After being submerged in the Land of Protruding Ribs for so long I had a craving for barbecue, I finally lost it when a salesgirl asked if she could help me.

"Honestly, it's useless, because you don't have my size, I need a fourteen, and I am a giant in your world," I said, throwing up my hands. "Apparently everyone who shops here is the size of a Kee-bler elf or a first-grader."

The salesgirl actually laughed, putting me a little at ease. "We do have other sizes," she said nicely. "Is that the dress you like? I can pull it from the back, where we keep our plus sizes."

Now, I didn't know whether to run or shove a Suzy-Q in her face in protest. The plus sizes? An eight was a plus size? Okay, sure, my size dress requires more material than say, a dress for an Olsen twin, but come on, it's not the size of a car! I suppose you can never be too careful, though; put a size-fourteen dress on a rack, and who would really be surprised if the whole fixture was just ripped right out of the wall and took an entire building down with it?

I left before the salesperson returned with the dress, even though I'm sure she had to hire several men right off the street and maybe a forklift to help her carry it. Even if that dress fit me perfectly, my Fat Money was not going to be burned there.

I learned a lesson that day, and that lesson was that if a store is too embarrassed to have me as a customer, if a store is too skinny to carry my size and display it out in public with the thinner, cuter sizes, then I'm too proud to give them my money. And I felt the same way in the store in Seattle.

Before I could say, "Meg! Let's get out of here, the only people who could fit into this stuff are junkies!" I turned around just in time to see her pluck a familiar aqua poplin day dress off the rack and head to the dressing room with it in one hand and Carmen in the other.

"I'm going to try this on," Meg giggled.

I nodded and smiled, trying to hide my dismay and encourage my friend to have fun at the same time. "I'll watch the baby while you're in the dressing room," I said.

The next boutique was the same—dresses that could only fit a pretzel stick (unsalted) or Meg—so I watched the baby after scouring the racks and finding many adorable things but none in my size. Finally, in subsequent stores that we visited, I didn't even bother with the clothes section of the store and headed straight for the "non-size" items, like body lotion and candles, and then just sat in front of the dressing room with Carmen until Meg was done. I should have brought some change to jingle in my pocket,

I thought; I have officially slipped into the role of The Guy on shopping expeditions, except for the part when other customers in the store would assume the adorable infant was mine. Then I'd have to explain, "No, she's my friend's baby," at which Meg would pop out of the dressing room and the other customer would gasp, "Oh! Yours? But you look so great!"

"You're not having any fun," Meg said sadly as we added another bag to her growing mountain of great, cool clothes finds. "You haven't bought one thing! We should just go home."

I realized then that Meg didn't know that we were visiting skinny-only stores, because Meg had been only one of two things in her life: skinny or pregnant. I mean, the girl thought that she was FAT simply because she finally filled something out, even if it was just her nursing bra.

"No, absolutely not," I replied. "We are not going home. You've been dying to go shopping for months! We're going to hit every store you want and you're going to buy fabulous things. I just haven't found . . . the perfect fit yet, that's all."

At the next store, I exploded with manufactured enthusiasm over a fig-scented candle, asked the salesgirl some pertinent and pointed questions about acne cream, and then held up a pair of underwear the size of a cocktail napkin and bellowed to Meg, "I have been driven MAD trying to find these!"

However, the angry little miss inside my head was having a field day all her own: You know, in California every restaurant has to post its health-inspection grade in the front window so the customers know exactly what they're getting into. If you'd like to go home with your intestines intact, you pick an A joint; if you have a decent co-pay and want some paid time off from work, choose option B; and if you're angling for long-term disability or an alternative to gastric bypass surgery, C is your way to go. The same should go for boutiques. I say, don't waste my time, just say what you are. Let me know right off if I have a better chance of fitting into something at Baby Gap than I do in your store. I want to see it posted in your front window: "Sizes Six and Under: For Paris Hilton, women with tapeworms, and young boys"; "Super Small Sizes: For Lara Flynn Boyle, political prisoners on hunger strikes, and everyone else 180 calories away from death"; and "Teeny-Weeny Sizes: For skeletons that hang in doctors' offices, mummies, and Prada models."

I have been a frequent visitor to sales racks in almost every major department and clothing store, and guess what's on them? XS's and S's. Size zeroes, twos, fours, and sixes. Rarely at Banana Republic will you spot a hallowed L on the sales rack, and ditto for J. Crew. The large sizes are always the first ones to get picked (for a change). Which tells me one thing: There's way more of us out here than there are of them, and they'd better watch it. Should we decide to declare war on them, well, my Fat Money is on the Fat Girls. We don't need bullets; all we need is to pass around a box of See's chocolates for some extra energy and then huff and then puff and then blow their bones down.

I mean, can it get any worse than this? Any worse than stores that house the larger-than-chic sizes away where no one can see them, or shops that simply just don't carry them at all? Will they become like the airlines and start weighing people at the door before they're allowed access? "Oh—a size fourteen? Hmmmm. Well, you, with your waterbed-like ass, take up as much room as two Lilliputian size zeroes. You'll have to wait until those attractive thin girls over there leave before you can come in. But don't you dare handle any of our stock too much. We don't want you passing the fat gene to our clothes, you size LARGE!!"

"Jeans?" Meg cried delightedly, and I suddenly realized that the little angry voice inside my head hadn't been completely contained there after all. "Did you find jeans? Did you find something cool to get? I knew you would find something here! This is my favorite store, you know!"

"Not yet, but I'm on a mission!" I assured her. "I'm sure this is the place."

While Meg met her match in the dressing room, I strolled around the shop with Carmen, desperate to find anything so Meg wouldn't feel so bad about me not being able to fit into a tank top the size of a panty liner. I finally sighed with relief when I spotted a lightweight butt body shaper with some pretty lace around each leg in the lingerie section. I flipped to the tag and nearly gasped. What I saw there nearly took my breath away and almost made me drop the baby: L. I saw an L. What on earth a girdle was doing in this shop I didn't know and I didn't care—it had probably been misordered and had sat there for years, been used as a dust rag, to stuff a couple bras, kill some bugs, who knew—but finally I was going to buy something and walk out with a bag of my own.

I raced up to the counter with the girdle and pulled out my credit card. The owner of the shop—a pretty, young, skinny-minnie girl with collarbones so prominent they could be used for rock climbing—picked it up, looked at it for a moment, and with a little laugh said, "Oh! This is NOT the right size for you!"

I smiled, excited, pleased, and humbled that she had mistaken me for a medium, since all she had really seen for such a long time were miniature-size people that she had absolutely forgotten what a real human looked like. "Oh," I said. "It's OK. That's a good size for me."

"No, really," the woman said, nodding vigorously. "You need an extra-large, and that's not a size we carry in the store regularly, but I can order it for you. I can have it here next week."

And then she tilted her skinny little head.

And then she smiled at me.

Even the girdle I wanted to buy was too small. The woman, that awful, awful woman, wouldn't even let me buy that stupid LARGE girdle. I WAS TOO FAT FOR THAT.

My face started burning around the edges and I didn't know what to say. I was stunned and embarrassed and mortified and I was FAT and I felt like I was in the seventh grade again and a cheerleader had just told me my pants were too tight and I had also just had my period in them.

"Should I order it?" the owner said.

"I don't think so," I finally said, looking right at her. "My fat ass doesn't live here."

Feeling as big as a Kodiak bear, I then sat down on the Skinny Store couch, mumbling something aloud about hoping that it could support my weight. I thought very, very hard about farting on it for a simple yet effective form of revenge, but then remembered I had an innocent baby in my presence and gracefully, though reluctantly, refrained (although I did not refrain from leaving a tiny wad of now flavor-depleted Bubble Yum underneath it).

But wait.

There are such things as happy endings, even for a size fourteen wandering the streets looking for a fabulous dress to take home. On my next trip to New York, I found Jill Anderson, a small boutique in the East Village that sells fantastic clothes in XS, S, and M, and then dares to put an L on a tag, too, and mean it. Not only was there a size fourteen dress right out there on the sales rack next to a six, a four, and a two, but there in that dress was room for my boobs, my butt, and my hips. I no longer felt like a Chernobyl monster. I felt like a girl and I felt pretty and I felt good. When Jill was named Best Women's Designer in New York by a prominent media outlet this year, my heart swelled with joy, not only for her, but for all of the L's out there who had finally found her at last.

Although there will never be world peace, I do find much comfort in that there is a place out there where size doesn't matter, where all that matters is that you're a girl (and sometimes that doesn't even matter so much because on one occasion, I was trying on the same dress that a man was, and it may be up for debate, but I will still argue to this day that I looked better in it than he did). Despite the shame of the "plus sizes" hidden away in stockrooms or the XL's that are only available by special order in other places in the universe, there is one place in the East Village where a size two and a size fourteen accidentally touched butts in a dressing room and war didn't break out. No one screamed and no one called the Fat HazMat team. They both laughed, the size fourteen was lacerated by the jutting hip bone of the size two, but after a little hydrogen peroxide and a Band-Aid, all was dandy and then the fourteen and the two told each other just how great they looked in their dresses. The cut scabbed over, but I'll always have that dress.

In the East Village at Jill's, we'll just wait until the rest of the world catches on.

That's Not Pudding

As much as I didn't want to think about it, I was getting mad. Standing in the checkout line at the bargain/closeout store, I was starting to seriously consider if ninety-nine-cent blank videotapes were worth this kind of hassle.

Let me say right now that when I initially entered the store, it seemed completely empty. There wasn't a soul around loading five-cent dented cans of fruit, expired dog food, or flammable toys that doubled as choking hazards in their shopping carts.

However, as soon as I grabbed the videotapes and headed for the cashier, I saw the beginnings of Swarm the Cashier Syndrome. The minute I approach the cash registers, people start to bum-rush the checkout lanes. It's almost as if the customers were bees and once they caught the scent of panic in the air, the fear that someone might get in line ahead of them, every single customer—even those who don't have anything in their baskets yet—will converge on the checkout lanes like pimps on a bus station.

It was instant bedlam, and though I risked being bowled over by a stroller pushed by a teen mom wearing a tank top that said in glitter letters, YOUR BOYFRIEND THINKS I'M HOT, I ducked into a line behind a blond lady.

I started feeling lucky that I had secured the second-in-line position until I looked ahead of me and saw the bounty that nested inside the blond lady's cart. Then again, I should have known.

When faced with the choice of lingering behind A) a lady who has enough stuff in her cart to identify her as either a Mormon, a Catholic, or a concession-stand owner, or B) a guy holding a six-pack, I'll make the obvious choice. Without a doubt, I'll still be standing there ten minutes later as the mother of twelve is loading her bagged groceries into her SUV and the guy with the six-pack is being wrestled to the floor and cuffed by store security.

Getting behind the blond lady was a colossal mistake. As I peered into her cart, I realized I hadn't seen that much crap since my work-related bridal shower, when everyone who came hated me and really only stayed for the cake. In that cart, there were a bunch of green candles shaped like a clover leaf, generic batteries, a bunch of pencils with little cats on them, and what looked like a breast pump. But the cashier hadn't even gotten to any of that crap yet. Instead, she was busy waiting for a price check on an ugly comforter that was also in the crap lady's cart.

To find a price, the cashier took the comforter from its plastic bag and held one side of it over her head, and as it unfolded, a round of disgusted gasps escaped from everyone in line.

There, on the stretched-out comforter, for everyone to see, was a massive poop stain the size of my arm that looked remarkably like the shape of Italy.

"Ewwwww!" I heard myself say. "That's not pudding."

Just then, another cashier announced that her line was open. Before I could even take a step, a lady four places behind me scurried over and threw her hoard of crap—including countless packages of fake nails, a rusted tube of Vagisil, and several mousetraps—on the counter. She had cut! I glared at the cutter lady as I walked over and stood behind her. The cashier rang up the nails and the traps and then looked for a price tag on a thermos set.

"I think that was $7.99," the cutter lady said. As soon as the cashier punched that amount in, the cheater cried, "Wait! It was $6.99!"

"Price check!" the cashier called over the intercom. And then we stood there. And stood there. And stood there. Finally, when the price-checker guy returned from Afghanistan, where he had apparently spent his fifteen-minute smoke break, he returned the verdict that the thermos was indeed $6.99.

"I knew it!" the cutter lady chortled with a grin and raised her fist in victory.

"I've already entered $7.99," the cashier said frantically. "Should I void out the whole thing?"

The thought of watching the whole fake-nail, mousetrap, and rancid-feminine-cream debacle unfold again in front of me was too much to bear. Honestly. I just couldn't do it. I simply couldn't allow it.

"What do I do?" the cashier cried out.

"I'm not paying $7.99 for that thermos," the cutter lady informed us.

"Here!!" I said to her and held out a dollar. "Just take it. *Take* it. Here's your dollar!"

The cutter lady looked at me like she had no idea she was an idiot, like she was unaware that she was a blight on society, that she was simply oblivious to the fact that she *was wasting my time for a frigging dollar.*

"TAKE IT!" I hissed as I shook the money in front of her face. "Take this and *go*. Go home, scratch your private parts with your fake nails, and kill some mice! Why not? Celebrate! You saved a whole dollar!"

I understand that I crossed a line, but I have to tell you that it felt *good*. I felt liberated, I felt free, even when the cheater plucked the dollar from my hand and left the store. In fact, I was still smiling when the cashier rang up my blank videotapes and said that the total was $4.27.

"Why, look at that," I said, counting the cash in my hand. "I'm a dollar short."

Spooker

"Oh, no," my husband said immediately as he walked through the front door. "Not again. I'm not doing this again!"

"But this time, it's real," I stressed.

"Every vision you have of the Apocalypse is real," he retorted. "Remember when you thought the Year 2000 bug was going to end the world and we had to stay home on New Year's Eve because you hadn't finished filling up every container you could get your hands on with water? Because of you I NEVER got to party like it was 1999!"

"It was for our own safety," I protested.

". . . And you bought those titanium bicycle helmets that we were supposed to wear all the time in case a meteor smacked us in the head?"

"It was a precaution," I argued.

". . . And you spent the house payment on forty cases of Ensure?" he continued. "What is it this time? What did you see? Did Oprah have Pat Robertson on again?"

I ran to the coffee table and presented my evidence, handing him the latest issues of my favorite alarmist magazines. "I got these in the mail today," I said sternly. "There are stories in this one about a volcano that's due to erupt and cause a huge mountain to fall into the ocean, creating a massive tidal wave that will flood the earth, and in this one there's a story about terrorists planning to blow up the Palo Verde Nuclear Plant, which, by the way, is the biggest in the country AND only about fifty miles from here! We're going to be like Chernobyl people, minus the babushkas and goats! We have to be prepared."

"So what is all of this?" he asked, pointing to the heap on the dining room table.

"Well," I said, mistaking his query for genuine interest, "this is the beginnings of our one-month food supply."

"We're supposed to live for a month off of this?" he said, looking over my rations. "All you have here is chocolate-covered raisins, Dots, and seven, eight boxes of Bugles!"

"I know," I agreed, throwing my hands up. "Walgreens was out of Funyons ALREADY! At least I was able to get the last of the Rad Block pills! There's a mushroom cloud on the label with a line through it!"

"Oh, as long as it has a line through it on the label, I'm sure it will really work. Is this . . ." my husband said, picking up one of the items from the table, "a breast pump? I'm not drinking that!"

"Don't be gross!" I cautioned. "That's a filter so we can turn our urine into water."

"I'm calling your mother," my husband said, reaching for the phone, "and we're sending you back to that doctor."

"Mom," I told her over the phone, "this problem is serious. Our world has many potential tragedies facing it today, don't you watch the news? You could strangle yourself on a drapery cord. Now this massive ice mountain is about to fall into the sea and generate a deadly tidal wave—and terrorists are going to melt the nuclear plant down. You need to start stocking up on food now!"

"Did you ever think," she replied, "that maybe JESUS IS COMING BACK? Don't worry about me. I've been to confession! But you've got enough sin on you to sink a ship, so if I were you, I'd leave the breast pump alone and go back to church! Besides, this whole thing was cooked up by Home Depot so we'll buy more duct tape!"

Honestly, though, this is from a woman who swears that the outtakes from *A Bug's Life* were real bloopers and that the government continually switches around the Fourth of July holiday so that it always falls on a three-day weekend.

"I'm telling you right now," she added, "don't you *dare* drink milk from yourself. That's disgusting, and it's a sin."

"You're right, Mom," I agreed. "We're getting a cow."

"What?" my husband yelled from across the room. "We have a blind dog and a toothless cat with rotting kidneys! No, you cannot have a cow. The last thing I want to do is wake up in the morning and step in a doody pie in the hallway as big as a hubcap."

"All right, we don't need a cow," I conceded, hanging up the phone. "A goat, then. If it worked in Chernobyl, it can work for us, plus I can save on lawn maintenance. I need to save every penny I can in an apocalyptic world."

"You just get freaked so fast," my husband said, trying to reason with me. "Year 2000 bug?"

Okay, fine, I admit it, I'm a spooker. I get spooked easily. During my preparations for the Year 2000 bug, I bought so many boxes of low-fat Pop-Tarts that Kellogg's decided not to discontinue them after all. When Safeway started accepting debit cards, I was convinced that it was only a matter of time before I would have my Mark of the Beast credit-card number tattooed on my forehead, and that I would eventually have to pledge my allegiance to Satan before I could buy a half-pound of tomatoes and some maple syrup.

This, however, is in NO WAY my fault. It all started when my parents sent me to church camp one summer and we watched a movie in which the people in it just vanished from their driver's seats, playgrounds, and work desks and just flew up into the sky. The people left on Earth then either got crucified on light poles and billboards or had their heads chopped off by Satan's storm troopers. It was a terrifying film, and I now realize that it's not something a twelve-year-old needs to see. My view is that it's okay to inform kids about maxi pads and STDs, but let's save the rapture movie for driver's ed or pay-per-view. After I came back from church camp, I spent the next six months wearing a Ziggy T-shirt that proclaimed I'M A C.O.G.! (Child of God) as insurance to get beamed up, and worrying that if my best friend didn't come to school that day, I had been left behind because my mom hadn't washed Ziggy the night before.

"Okay, okay," I said to my husband as he picked up a food dehydrator off the table and shot me a look. "Maybe I did get carried away. Maybe the world won't end in a year, maybe it won't end until 2028, when the Aztec calendar stops."

"The Bugles will be very old by then," my husband said. "They will have lost their snappy crunch."

"They weren't to eat," I said. "They were to put on our fingers and poke the eyes out of looters."

"I'm taking them back," he said. "And I'm taking the remaining cases of Ensure back, too."

"You know, when your intestines are hanging out of your butt because of massive radiation exposure," I shouted, "you're really going to wish you had a nice can of Ensure to pass through your contaminated digestive system!"

"You know," my husband said as he stopped and looked at me, "if my bowels are dragging on the ground, I highly doubt that the first thing on my mind is going to be a light liquid snack."

When he returned from Walgreens, he had a present for me. "Here," he said as he handed over a copy of *Glamour*. "There's nothing about the Apocalypse in the table of contents. If you have to read a magazine, read this."

I flipped through it quickly, and then I stopped, gasped, and pointed.

"What?" my husband said. "There's nothing about the fallen mountain flood in it, is there?"

"No," I laughed, flipping the magazine over so he could see. "But I bet a couple of months after the nuclear plant blows up, I will *finally* be this skinny."

Head Over Heels

When I saw the flashing lights come up behind me, I hardly should have been surprised.

While I truly didn't believe I deserved a ticket for what I had just done, something was certainly due to me. For the past twenty minutes I had been circling the crowded downtown Phoenix streets on none other than St. Patrick's Day, trying to find my drunk husband, which was no easy task. Even when sober, my darling husband is nothing short of a submarine without sonar in the ocean of life, constantly bobbing around on nothing more than mere hopes that he'll eventually bump into where he's supposed to be.

"I'm on Second Avenue and Monroe," my husband said as he called from his cell phone a half an hour ago. "We'll be waiting on the corner."

As I circled that corner for the third time, I realized I would have had better luck finding the gum that might have fallen out of his mouth somewhere on the sidewalk, because at least that would have stayed put. It didn't help that his rendezvous point was the precise location of the biggest Irish bar in town, which had pretty much stopped being a bar that day and had been transformed into a street fair.

People were everywhere, staggering this way and that, much as if the Betty Ford Clinic's security staff had gone on strike and the streets were suddenly inundated by free-range substance abusers on holiday. Not that I haven't been a free-range substance abuser myself on several occasions, but when I'm driving, the last thing I need is a herd of inebriates darting in and out of traffic like loaded chickens. I don't exactly possess the skills of an air traffic controller, and what little radar I do have really needed to be concentrated on finding my husband, not on hoping that the bump I just hit in the road was a big sack of flour and not a St. Paddy's Day reveler whom I'm married to. This is precisely why I refuse to operate a cell phone when behind the wheel: I simply do not possess the necessary skills to pay attention to the road and take on an additional motor activity, and from the looks of it, neither does anyone else out there barreling down the street in their Yukon XL and gossiping about other preschool mothers at the same time. Maybe it takes a self-esteem healthier than my own, but I simply cannot fathom thinking that as the operator of a multi-ton death machine, I am talented, gifted, and remarkable enough to put the car on autopilot for the duration of the impromptu performance of "And That's Why I Don't Talk to Her That Much Anymore" in the sole hope that in the moment it takes to avert a tragedy, I will suddenly transform into MacGyver and tip the battering ram up on two wheels to avoid, say, a free-range substance abuser making a mad dash for some green beer. You know, I wouldn't consider handling my Weedwacker and flossing shredded beef out of my teeth at the same time, two pastimes that not only need but deserve whatever focus your ADD syndrome hasn't already destroyed, and there's far less danger involved there. Even if the floss gets caught on the bottom edge of my crown and a struggle ensues, there's little to no chance that my Weedwacker will end up wrapped around a pole or that I'll be wearing a tiara of shattered glass when the dust settles. Most people have enough difficulty driving as it is; throwing in another variable is beyond me, and, personally, I think it requires so much ability, dedication, and plain raw talent to pull off successfully that it should probably be designated an Olympic event and kept exclusively there.

Now, that said, after the third lap around the corner in question, I had had it. I was furious with my husband for not being where he was supposed to, for drinking enough that he couldn't drive, but mainly for getting drunk without me. I knew I was never going to find him on my own, so I did the unthinkable. At a red light, while the car was NOT moving, I pulled out my cell phone, out of pure desperation. And I called him.

"WHERE ARE YOU?" I bellowed into the phone. "I've circled that corner THREE TIMES and you are not on Second Avenue and Monroe. You are the only drunk person in Phoenix not on that corner, you know."

"I'm on Second Street and Monroe," my husband replied.

"Oh my God, green light, I'm moving," I said as the traffic light switched and I suddenly found myself in an intersection about to turn left. "I have to go."

"Wait! Second Street, honey! I'll be waving!" my husband said.

"Fine," I answered, and considering the line of cars behind me, made a move on the left turn as an opening in traffic approached, but, as I was completing the maneuver, two free-rangers jumped into the crosswalk and attempted to run across the street as my car turned in front of them. As I was a good ten feet away from them, I was in no danger of catapulting either one over my hood like a shot put, but I was not surprised when the flashing lights lit up my rearview mirror like a Christmas tree.

I had my registration, insurance card, and license in hand before the officer even got to the window.

Personally, I think I deserved a ticket simply for being on the phone and breaking my oath to myself. But, more important, I have been *owed* that ticket, and much more, for almost a decade.

First, you need to understand something.

Phoenix summers are so incredibly hot you can't imagine them. They are unbearably hot. They're so hot that should you find yourself in this hellhole in July and you don't have any escape money, you should know that a parking space in the shade is worth more than your car's weight in gold, and people have been known to physically fight over them. You should NEVER fall asleep in the sun, since you will not fully understand the meaning of "mercy killing" until you've experienced a full-body Phoenix sunburn. If you step outside barefoot, kiss half your ass good-bye, because it will be used to resole your feet. If you forget or misplace your driving mitts, your socks or a pair of maxi pads (the kind with the sticky strips) will act as nice substitutes. Never, EVER touch the handle of a shopping cart unless you have proof it's been in the store for at least an hour and has completely returned to its former state as a solid. Look before you sit; remember that a coin exposed to sunlight on a car seat for more than forty seconds ceases being pocket change and becomes a branding iron once it makes contact with the skin on the back side of your leg.

And, finally, if you decide to take a fun day trip or hike into the desert with a group of friends, just expect someone to wander off and die. We lose a person a week just in picnics alone.

Summers are merciless.

It was a July about nine years ago and I was working at a tiny little magazine my friends and I had started. Our "office" was in a former motel, which now housed, in addition to our endeavor, a telemarketing firm that sold knives and other sharp weapons and was eventually raided by the ATF, and a "photography" studio downstairs that saw most of its business after midnight. The rent was cheap, and for good reason. With a porn factory downstairs and a machete pusher across the hall, it's clear that our address didn't reflect the pedigree of a Trump Tower. In addition, more frequently than not, the air-conditioner was nothing but a faint memory, and on those unfortunate occasions when it was 118 outside, it was 118 inside, too.

It was one of those miserable, air-conditionerless days when if you sat still long enough without a drink of water, you could watch yourself begin to mummify. Someone mentioned sno-cones, and I volunteered immediately because I had air-conditioning in my car and I had sweated so much over my keyboard that the keys were sticking. Off I went around the corner with the sno-cone order in my hand. I had just turned the steering wheel and was making sure traffic was clear when I heard an odd noise, as if someone had thrown a rather large potato at my car, and when I looked up, there was a man. On the other side of my windshield, his head parallel to my head, his hands on the glass on either side of his face. There was a man. His mouth wide open, his eyeballs took on the size of hard-boiled eggs, and he was just sprawled on my car, all over the hood. It was like I was at an aquarium and all of a sudden there was a merman. He stayed there for a second, and when I stopped the car, he slid backward, his hands squeaking against the hood of my car, and then he fell off.

"What a nutjob! Are you crazy?" I actually cried out loud, and I looked past the man, now burning his exposed skin on the pavement, and saw a bike on the ground, the wheels still spinning.

"Why are you jumping on my car if you already have a ride? You scared me half to death!" I continued, and then I understood as people from all over began to gather around him and help him up.

Then it hit me.

Holy shit.

I just hit him.

Holy shit. HOLY SHIT! I just hit a guy. I just hit THAT GUY who rolled off my car like a giant Hickory Farms summer sausage. Where did he come from? How did this happen? I didn't even see him! Am I sure that I hit him? Maybe he really did just jump on my car! I can't believe this! Did this really happen or is he a bad heat mirage? My car wasn't even moving! How could I have possibly hit him?

I didn't know what to do, so I sat there for a moment, just in shock, and then shut off the car.

"Oh, shit!" I yelled as I ran over to him. "Are you okay? *Are you okay!*"

With the help of some passersby, the man stood up and dusted himself off, then picked his still-spinning bike up from the street, and the cowboy hat I had apparently knocked right off his head. I felt horrible. I felt like such a monster for hitting someone with a stationary car.

"Are you okay?" I asked the man again. "I didn't even see you until we were eye-to-eye, when you landed on my car! I thought you were a potato! I'm so sorry! I really am sorry! Can I help you, are you hurt?"

"I okay," he said with a nod. "I okay." Then he pointed to the bike. "Okay. Okay. I okay."

"Really? Are you sure? Do you want me to call someone, an ambulance?" I insisted.

The man kept shaking his head and held on to the bike.

"What we really should do is call the police," a nosy bystander who had been waiting for the bus said.

Before I could step forward and say, "Um, excuse me, this is OUR accident, *his and mine,* and we don't really need any input from you, *bus person,* you don't even drive a car, so what would you know about hitting somebody, *anyway?*" my victim started shaking his hand and became visibly alarmed.

"No, no, no, no police," he repeated. "No police! I okay, I okay, I okay!"

Clearly, the man had issues with the police, and frankly, I was no fool, I didn't want the police poking around either. I mean, not only was I looking at a rate hike in my insurance for tossing a bicyclist, but there may have even been potential for something as unthinkable as jail time, or even driving school.

"We should call the police," the bus person declared again, which was enough to send my victim into something of a meltdown.

"*Por favor, por favor*, no police," he begged. "No police!"

"Are you not a citizen?" I said to him quietly through clenched teeth, but he looked at me as if he had no idea what I was saying. "Illegal? Are you illegal?"

Well, I might as well have just flashed him a badge that said INS, because the poor man, despite the fact that he had just been hit, albeit lightly—it would really be more concise to say he was simply tapped—by a car, got on his piece-of-shit, broken, dented, and mangled bike and sped away like he was Lance Armstrong.

"Good job," I said to the bus person as I nodded at her. "That was a good move. I was just about to get him a sno-cone!"

Ever since, I have felt terrible about questionably hitting that illegal alien on a bike, but if I may be honest, if you're going to smack someone with your car on the way to get a sno-cone, or they are going to smack you, it's sadly preferable to have one who's about an arm's length on the other side of the law. Especially when his punishment would have been way worse than mine had the authorities been on the scene. I'd gladly take jail time and spend my days picking up trash in an orange jumpsuit on the side of the road over living in Mexico, most of which makes some Indian reservations look like Hilton Head by comparison. At least in jail I'd have air-conditioning and basic cable and I probably wouldn't have to eat my pet.

So that is why, when I saw the flashing lights behind me, I had everything in place and handed it over to the officer, did not beg for a warning, and gladly accepted a ticket for NOT hitting those people in the crosswalk in lieu of the one who had already landed on the hood of my car like he was a part from the Space Shuttle. The cop was very nice, especially when he understood that my anger toward my husband was a good indication of my sobriety, in addition to the fact that I made no attempt to hug him when he handed me my ticket.

"Just be a little careful about those crosswalks," the cop reminded me. "You can turn after the pedestrians have passed you, but don't turn in front of them. That will get you another ticket."

"I can tell you I'll be very, very careful," I said. "I promise I'll never do that again."

"And make sure you watch out for bikers, they can pop out of nowhere," the cop told me. "Just keep a head's up."

"You know," I agreed, "I couldn't have said it better."

eBaby

When my sister asked me to teach her how to bid on eBay, I hesitated for a moment.

"No," I replied. "No, I can't do it. I'm sorry, I can't tell you."

"What?" she cried. "Why can't you tell me?"

"Because," I said, taking a deep breath, "you have a family. You have a job. You're too green, you won't be able to handle it."

"That is the dumbest thing I've ever heard," she retorted. "It's *eBay*. Every moron and their mother is on it!"

"Precisely," I told her firmly. "Listen, it's for your own good. It's not what you think. Once you bite into the eBay pie, nothing ever tastes the same."

"Fine, then, I'll figure it out myself," she threatened, backing me into a corner.

I couldn't let her wander into that terrain alone; eBay is a strange, magical, and dangerous place where the enchanting dance of bidding and outbidding can twist up your common sense and willpower like a pretzel until you no longer have a shred of self-control and your id is running rampant.

At first, to a novice, eBay seems a land of possibilities with no horizon; anything is possible, everything you ever wanted is available, and it's all for sale. Any toy that never made it under the Christmas tree because your parents were too frugal and didn't give a shit about breaking your nine-year-old heart that had never yearned for anything so deeply as it did the Sunshine Family dolls and their easily assembled Sunshine Family Craft Store and Organic Vegetable Stand, well, it's all there on eBay. All of it. The Sunshine Family Mom, the Sunshine Family Dad, their baby, and the vegetable stand from which they earned their wholesome living, growing the produce themselves and selling it to Barbie, Holly Hobbie, and the Bionic Woman (who, although she was supposedly robot from the waist down, was a bit of a tart and curiously "lost" her pants the first day my sister got her).

If the Bionic Woman was so inclined and had by now made the realization that her slutty ways and their result—the Sunshine Family divorce—had gotten her nowhere but to a garage sale with "25 cents" written on masking tape and slapped across her naked thighs, she could buy her pants back on eBay, too.

The Marc Jacobs boots I became utterly obsessed with because I was too cheap to buy them retail until they were all gone and I finally understood I was willing to trade a kidney for them if need be. It took seven months of searching on eBay, seven months of scouring the listings every single day until I finally found them, cheap as dirt, shown in their original box and a size too small, but they were mine and I still had a kidney to swap.

The circa-1900 cast-iron Christmas tree stand that cost forty bucks to ship and could only accommodate the tiny trunk of a poor pioneer family's Christmas sapling; not one logged from a redwood forest and sold by Home Depot.

A charming old folk painting of a buxom nude woman that my husband refuses to let me hang up due to the artist's inability to conquer the complexities of the human hand, although he was quite expert at rendering claws. Subsequently, he gave his subject two lobsterlike appendages, causing my husband to exclaim, "Would you just cover the damn thing up? It's like looking at a portrait of Anna Nicole Scissorhands. Every time I see it I get an overwhelming desire to put on a bib, melt some butter, and suckle a claw."

The two-foot-tall vintage garden gnome that I prepared a prestigious spot in my garden for, only to be quite saddened when it arrived packed in a jewelry box since it was two inches, not two feet, tall.

It's all there for the bidding, plus 567 other things that I've bought.

And that was a door I could not bring myself to open for my sister. I simply couldn't bear the responsibility.

"Listen," I said frankly, "I can't be a party to this. It would be like jumping you into a gang. The first day, it's great, you're walking around in a brand-new world, you bid on the Sunshine Family and before you know it, it's two A.M. and you're counting down the seconds until an auction ends so you can snipe someone named "KewtiePie" for a Lizzie Borden Living Dead Doll, not because you want it—you already have two of them somewhere in a pile in a closet—but because she outbid you earlier in the day, the stupid little asshole! Because that's what you get when you mess with the master! *You get sniped* and I *win*. I WILL ALWAYS WIN. You're up in the middle of the night trying to swipe a doll away from what was probably a sixth-grader, *just because you can*. I'm your sister, not your dealer. I *just can't do that to you*."

My sister, still not sensing the magnitude of danger she was about to encounter, embarked on the journey solo. Although I felt bad, I knew she needed to find her own way. In a couple of days, it was all too evident what sort of danger she was involving herself in.

"Guess what I just bought?" she would call and ask. "I just bought purple Jimmy Choo size-twelve shoes for a hundred dollars that the mom in *Daddy Day Care* wore! I'm going to sell these again on eBay and I'm going to make a mint!"

"I think you'd better focus on trying to find a new friend with a

Stevie Nicks sense of style and the feet of a lumberjack," I replied. "Or a cross-dresser."

"Someone just outbid me!" she would call and exclaim. "So I just sent them an e-mail telling them how *rude* they are! I was there first!"

"If you were outbid on the pantyhose, bra, or underwear that the mom or anyone else wore in *Daddy Day Care*, e-mail them back and thank them," I suggested.

"My Jimmy Choo *Daddy Day Care* shoes still haven't come in the mail!" she later called and cried. "I'm going to leave that seller negative feedback right now! It's been *three days*!"

"Okay, you know what?" I finally said. "You need to chill out. I have been on eBay for five years, and you're the kind of person on it that I hate. The new people who waddle around and spaz out, outbidding someone every time someone outbids them instead of sitting back and playing the game. There should be an eBay wading pool where you only get to bid on Precious Moments figurines and Avon products and you have to make it through *that* first before jumping into the deep end. Do you know what you are?"

"Shut up," my sister said.

"You're an EBABY," I informed her. "An EBABY! You paid a hundred bucks for purple giant shoes, people are always going to outbid you, and if you start giving people negative feedback for no reason, they're going to give it to you. Just be cool. Don't freak out!"

"I am not an eBaby," my sister replied quietly. "I have a feedback of three. Seven more and I get a star by my name."

My sister didn't call again, and I assumed she was taking my hard-earned advice. I hadn't heard from her in a couple of days when I got an e-mail from eBay saying that during a routine inspection, my personal information could not be verified. As a result, my user privileges on the site were suspended until I reentered that exact information in the designated space.

I did so hurriedly, submitted it as requested, but then nothing happened. No confirmation popped up, no verification, just a Web page with an error message on it.

I was puzzled for a moment, and then I gasped.

I had been had.

Even though it looked identical to an eBay page, right down to the logo and the copyright, it was a fake e-mail, the kind you get from people who want your information, like your user name and password, so they can access other information, like your credit-card numbers.

I immediately went to the real eBay page and changed my user ID, changed my password, then picked up the phone and dialed my sister's number.

"Did you get an e-mail from eBay asking for your user name and password?" I said, panicked that scalawags were now roaming about the Internet armed with my sister's Visa number.

"No, I don't think so," she said. "But even if I did, I wouldn't give them any information. It's all a scam."

"Oh," I replied simply. "Good."

"Why? Did you get an e-mail like that?" she asked.

"Sort of," I said. "But it looked just like eBay, with the logo and copyright and everything! It *looked* just like eBay!"

"You gave them your password, didn't you!" my sister demanded. "You fell for it!"

"I didn't *fall* for it," I said defensively. "It said I was suspended! What was I supposed to do? I bet a lot of people did just what I did!"

"Sure," my sister answered smugly. "Of course they did. Do you know what you are?"

"Shut up," I cried.

"EBABY!" she shot.

National Stupidity Day

❧

Somehow I must have missed the announcement on the news, but apparently everyone but me knew that it was a holiday.

It must have been. I can find no other explanation for what I encountered yesterday except that everybody gave their brain a day off in honor of National Stupidity Day.

Within three and a half minutes of leaving my house, I experienced so many stupid people that I'm positive I must have broken a record for something. The first stupid person I was exposed to was the guy in front of me in the right-hand lane on Sixteenth Street. He came to an abrupt and screeching halt as soon as the light turned green to let a mid-1970s Lincoln Continental, filled with what could only be pimps, into traffic from a gas station. The pimp driving the Lincoln qualified for my second stupid person encounter, as he tried to maneuver his cattle car of an automobile into the right-hand lane, an operation so intricate and it took him so long that the light turned red, and then he promptly ran it.

When I finally pulled into FedEx, my destination, there was a whole glob of stupidity waiting for me there, as well. A split microsecond before I had checked the last box on the address slip and was to take the final step I needed to be served next, an operative of stupidity suddenly popped up in front of me and captured my rightful place in line. It was 5:52 P.M.; FedEx closes at 6:00; and it was essential that my package get to New York before 10 A.M. the next day. I had already been impeded by a Random & Ignorant Act of Whirled Peas advocate in the car in front of me and the selfish, red-light-running pimp, both of whom had put me *dangerously* behind schedule.

Now, at FedEx, a whole new door to stupidity was about to open right before my eyes. The operative stepped up to the counter and said to the FedEx girl (and I quote EXACTLY):

"I sent a package from here and I was wondering if you knew where it was."

To which the FedEx girl replied, "What was the date you sent it?"

STUPIDITY OPERATIVE: "I'm not real sure."

FEDEX GIRL: "Do you have your tracking slip?"

SO: "Yes. What's that?"

FEG: "The slip you filled out that has the tracking number on it."

SO: "Oh. No, then, I guess not."

FEG: "Did you send it last week or the week before?"

SO: "Yes. Maybe."

FEG: "Which week?"

SO: "The week before. Maybe."

FEG: "What day of the week was it?"

SO: "I can't tell. Do you have a calendar?"

(This is the point in the scene where a new character, shifting her weight from foot to foot, sighing and rolling her eyes, whispers comments very loudly, mainly because, alarmingly, she has lost her fear of yelling at strangers.)

LAURIE NOTARO: "Does anyone here have a very sharp pencil? Anyone? Because I thought that jabbing it into my right eye has

GOT to be less painful than watching Twenty Questions With the Girl Who Has a Brick for a Brain."

FEG: "I don't have a calendar here, I'm sorry."

SO: "Okay. It was a weekday."

FEG: "Do you remember who helped you?"

SO: "You did! Do you remember what day it was?"

LAURIE NOTARO (to no one in particular): "Hi. I mailed a package here in 1989, or was it 1986, well, I think it was when Donald Reagan was still president, and I just wanted to check on it. You remember me, don't you?"

FEG: "Well, the computer can't start locating anything more than seven days old without a tracking number. I'm sorry."

SO: "Well, how am I supposed to find the package?"

FEG: "Locating your tracking slip would be a good first step."

SO: "I can't believe you won't help me. I thought UPS people were nice! I thought UPS people HELPED people!"

(Stupidity Operative then marches off in a huff and proceeds to the parking lot, where her boyfriend and their dirty baby, wearing only a diaper, are waiting for her in a corroding, formerly red Ford Escort with gray primer fenders and a bumper attached to the frame with duct tape. It is there that she will absolutely have a massive cow.)

LAURIE NOTARO: Wait! Come back, Brick-Brained Girl! I totally want to fight you! Come on, in the name of all that is stupid! Please?!!!

Now, I wish I could say this was the end of my Stupidity Day festivities, but it wasn't. I did learn, however, that if I ever decided to run for public office, I only needed one platform to win: Send all stupid people to Stupid Jail. Frankly, I can't fathom deriving any more joy than being able to step up to the Brick-Brained Girl, flash my badge and turn on my handheld siren (you really would need both, because the stupid won't understand you any other way), and say, "Ma'am, please come with me. You're under arrest for your flagrant display of extreme stupidity. Kiss your dirty baby good-bye. You won't see her again until she's sharing a cell with you. And that's a stupid car, so I'm impounding that, too."

See, that would be something I really could celebrate.

The Midas Touch

I get into a lot of bad trouble with my car, and I always wish that I had taken some kind of auto-repair class in high school instead of ceramics. In the course of my car-driving life, I have completed the impossible. I have driven my car up onto a median so far that three tires floated above the ground. I have forgotten to pull the parking brake, which caused my car to roll into the middle of the street in the dead of night until some policeman came and pushed it back and then told my dad. I have decapitated a total of three driver's-side mirrors, lopped off by a particularly evil mailbox while pulling out of my driveway. I have driven over at least seven concrete bumpers in about ten seconds during a rainstorm when my glasses had fogged up in a parking lot and I was on a date. A pebble once lodged itself in the brakes, causing such an agonizing metal-on-metal screech that pedestrians in the vicinity turned around to determine where the screaming noise was coming from.

In the course of this history, inevitably, I get taken by a mechanic or a service shop. It even happens every time I get my car fixed or oil changed and the golden egg of a dirty air filter pops its grimy head up and demands a replacement. It's a game. I realized this when my sister mentioned that her air filter also needed changing every time her oil did. My other sister agreed. So did my mother. But my father, husband, and brother-in-law just laughed at us, informing all of us girls that the dirty air filter was a trick. Personally, I think self-defense classes, particularly for women, should institute programs for protection in these situations.

"Ma'am, your air filter is mighty clogged up. Would you like to change it?"

Prepare the battle stance, knees locked, arms up and elbows bent, fists clenched. Step forward, throw a punch, scream, "NO!"

"Miss, the heels on the boots of your tires need renailing."

"NO!"

"Lady, the teeth on your flywheel all need root canals and capping."

"NO!!"

The last time an oil filter was presented to me, it was dripping ooze, looking as if it had been caught like a seagull in a tidal wave from the Exxon Valdez. I shook my head, and informed the mechanic that it looked just fine to me.

He stared at me, speechless, his fingers tightening along the oily rim, wondering to himself if I had recently sustained a massive crowbar injury to my head. "Whatever you say, lady," he snapped, which in Mechanic Speak means "You stupid broad. Women's libber!"

So when I gently bumped into a concrete parking slab while running an errand a couple of weeks ago and my car began to scream, I began to worry. It was a loud, high-pitched "Mommy-you're-hurting-me" kind of scream. I drove the car to the closest repair shop, which was a Midas, and Danny, the pudgy-bellied manager, pulled my car into the auto bay and put his guys right to work. Fifteen minutes later, he entered the waiting room, laughing. "I have good news for you," he said with a grin. "You'll never guess what that sound was!"

"A pebble," I said quietly.

"How did you know?" he inquired.

"It doesn't matter," I answered. "Is the car ready?"

"Well, that was the good news," he continued. "Your master cylinder needs to be replaced. I can have the part here in an hour. You car will basically fall apart without it."

"How much?" I said, my worst fears confirmed.

"It'll be three hundred and fifty dollars," Danny replied. "The gravity of the situation demands immediate action. I wouldn't drive from here to your house without getting this fixed first."

I clenched my fists, took a step forward, and whispered, "No."

"We have a payment plan," he added. "And I'll give you a ride back to your office."

Sucker.

Danny led me to his car, a fiery-red Camaro with black stripes, and I stood there, about to break the last in a set of rules I had made for myself when I was sixteen. Never wear sweatpants in public. Don't eat more than 800 calories a day. Don't throw your gauchos away, they will never go out of style. Never accept a ride in a Camaro.

I thought that rule was almost flagrant, as I never knew anyone who had actually owned one, and had heard several years ago that the grand chariots of White Trash Culture were no longer going to be produced. Not only did it make my heart skip a beat, it made me shout out loud that there must be a God after all.

And if that wasn't enough good news, the Pontiac Firebird was also being pulled from the lineup, though I suspect that either the Christ or his mother, Mary, tired and weary from decades of hanging from the rearview mirror and emitting a new-car smell, had something to do with that. Honestly, standing with Danny next to his car, I realized that I probably hadn't even *seen* a Camaro or Firebird since the last time I drove out of my high school parking lot, but I attributed their absence to the fact that all the guys who drove them knocked up their teen girlfriends and had to buy cars that would accommodate a baby. Like a Chevy crew-cab pickup.

It turns out that I was probably just living in the wrong part of town, which finally gives me something good to say about my neighborhood, even though most of my fellow residents wouldn't even consider a baby car seat. After all, why put a big, bulky thing in the backseat when ten other people need to sit back there, too?

Anyway, the announcement that the Camaro and Firebird species had a date with extinction couldn't be met with more pleasure from me. In fact, I do recall yelping out in glee when I heard the proclamation over the radio. If they're doing away with the Camaro, I thought then, the dark days of our civilization are definitely behind us. The potential for progress is enormous—I mean, if they quit making the Camaro, the days are numbered for Journey and White Snake rock blocks. It was a golden hope for a new society! Frankly, I had lost all faith in humankind, but it gave me confidence that we actually are progressing and evolving in an upwardly fashion. Besides, the Camaro culture has never been the same since guys stopped wearing corduroy shorts and tank tops made out of netting, anyway.

However, as I lowered myself to ground level and rather rolled into Danny's bucket seats, I understood that there was one sad orphan when we lost the Camaro and Firebird: A roach clip just doesn't look as good in, say, a Saturn or a Rav 4.

The next morning on my way to work, my Grand Master Flash Cylinder fixed, the sin of riding in a Camaro never to be washed from my history, I passed Midas. Standing out in front on the sidewalk were two men, one holding a cluster of balloons and the other a huge hand-painted picket sign that read THE MIDAS TOUCH CAN KILL YOU.

I didn't stop to ask, I didn't want to know. I wouldn't exactly have agreed, but certainly I knew, a little pure part of me that was once so proud was now quite dead, never to return.

Drive to Survive

When I entered the classroom for the driving school, I seriously debated if a warrant for my arrest due to noncompliance with my traffic ticket was better or worse than sticking it out for the whole day.

I just didn't know. Already it looked miserable. There, forty-five people in front of me in the registration line, was the best cross section of humanity any sociologist has ever seen. Included in this nuts-and-soft-center assortment were: a Paris Hilton wannabe, her explicitly low-cut porno jeans resting just below her hipbones, which stuck out like doorknobs; her friend, who stood next to her on six-inch-tall wedgie flip-flops as they chatted away, possibly unaware that they were signing up for eight hours of driver's ed and not an open cattle call for a reality show; the old, ancient man with crazy Grandpa Munster eyebrows who was clearly involved in some deep REM sleep despite his upright position; and the tall, burly guy with a meticulously trimmed mustache who assumed the "I'm pissed" stance and who I would have guessed to be a cop had he not been in this class.

After about ten minutes, I was pleasantly shocked and delighted when it was revealed that I wouldn't have to wait long to see my first show. The woman in front of me, who was shaped like an oil drum and looked as if raccoons had just dug through her hair searching for a snack, was the first to melt down.

"Here you go, sir," she said compliantly to the instructor as she stepped forward and handed him a copy of her traffic violation.

"Mmm-hmmm," he replied starkly, then looked up at her. "And the hundred-twenty-dollar fee, acceptable in a money order only?"

"Oh, sir," the barrel said, "I chose to be on time here this morning over stopping at the ATM."

"Well, that wasn't very smart," the instructor rebuffed. "You chose to come on time to a class you haven't even paid for, so I suggest—"

"OH PLEASE, SIR," the woman actually bellowed in a gutteral, deep, desperate howl, typically only heard on the Discovery Channel when a mother watches her offspring get eaten. "PLEASE! Please don't turn me away! I have to be in this class today, because I'm a trucker and if you turn me away, that's my liveihood, sir! That's the way I make a living, and if I don't take this class today I'll lose my license! And then I'll have nothing! It's my life, sir!"

"You got this ticket a month ago," the instructor, who in this line of work clearly had heard it all before, said. "You haven't driven past or seen an ATM in that whole time?"

The barrel stopped for a moment, searching, searching, searching, but obviously couldn't find a comeback, so she returned to her comfort zone of shameless begging.

"Oh please, sir, please, sir, I got in last night at four A.M., dropped off my load at Wal-Mart, got two hours sleep, and then came here. I've got to be in New Mexico tomorrow, so I really have to be in this class," the trucker explained, and, honestly, I did start to feel a little sorry for her, and at least sleeping in a truck explained her lack of attention to detail when it came to her grooming skills. Believe me, no one's going to mistake the back of my head for Nicole Kidman's, but if I had to freshen up at truck-stop restrooms as a matter of routine, I'd skip the hairdo procedure, too, in favor of not catching a venereal disease or quite possibly the whole rainbow of them by touching the faucet.

"On your allotted forty-minute lunch break I strongly suggest you make a trip to Circle K and get yourself a money order," he said sharply. "Or you won't be making any more trips anywhere."

"Thank you, sir, thank you, sir," the barrel replied, backing away and, oddly, bowing at the same time, as if she had just had an audience with King Solomon or the Pope. I was torn between yelling at her, "You come back here right now and kiss his ring!" and "Stop that! You're giving this ordinary city employee a false sense of power that will increase the chances of him abusing it for the next eight hours of this class!" I was afraid, however, that that might be just enough to make the barrel bond to me for the rest of the class and therefore make her unshakable, since the extent of her human contact was apparently rather limited. I took that time, instead, to keep my mouth shut and scout out a seat far away from the one where the barrel plopped down.

Aside from angering the emperor by handing him my traffic ticket instead of laying it flat, I escaped mostly unscathed and found a seat on an aisle and waited for class to start. I had already heard the rumblings of the "So what did you do?" conversations, in which each offender (particularly the males in this class) tried to outrank each other on the renegade traffic scale by going the fastest or brazenly running a red light. For people such as myself and everybody else in this class who is too chickenshit not to show up for traffic school, this is the pinnacle opportunity to exercise criminal bragging rights, since most likely speeding two miles over the limit in a school zone is the most horrible offense average citizens ever make, unless, naturally, one day we kill our spouse. Regular career criminals don't have the time, patience, or need to go to traffic school, because chances are when they got pulled over, there were either several kilos of cocaine, a couple of stolen DVD players, or the remains of a victim in the trunk.

Frankly, no one took the trouble to ask me why I was doing time in class, and I was a little bit relieved. Although I would fall to the bottom of the heap in the pecking order with the badass red-light runners by confessing, "Oh, it's silly. I was on a cell phone and wasn't paying attention, so I entered a crosswalk whilst pedestrians were occupying it," I was prepared to bring out the big guns if needed. So far, I apparently looked harmless enough not to be considered as competition, but should it come to that, I was ready. I was totally ready to break out, "Yeah, there was that thing with the crosswalk, whatever. But that's not what this is really about, you know. What I'm doing time for really in Karma Speak is hitting an illegal alien on a bike ten years ago, tossing him like a Frisbee onto my hood, and watching him peddle away on his mangled Husky three-speed because *somebody* mentioned something about deportation," because if I had to, I would. I *would*.

Finally, the class started and before we had even turned the first page in our workbooks, the Pissed-Off Guy raised his hand.

"Let me ask you something," he said without the instructor even seeing him. "I'm making a left-hand turn, right, and the guy in front of me goes on the yellow, but he waits too long so I have to go on the red, I see the photo radar flash for 'running the red' and a cop pulls behind me and writes me a ticket. I got two tickets, and I didn't even deserve *one!*"

Oh, no, I thought, we've made a remarkably early groundbreaking start on the "I Did Not Deserve This Ticket and I Was Wronged" segment, which I deplore. Honestly speaking, this is not my first time in traffic school but my second, although considering it's my second ticket in twenty years, I hardly consider myself a driving menace. Well, unless I'm on a cell phone, when only the people at least up on the second or third floors or those on roller skates are safe. Anyway, the point is that I'm familiar with the attempts of fellow classmates to try their "case" in front of the class and the teacher by telling their story, and I've never really been sure why. Even if the instructor, on a chance slimmer than a vomiting Olsen twin, agrees with you, he is not going to dismiss your ticket, mainly because he's *not a judge*. He's not going to let you walk out of class and let you have your Saturday back because, well, he's *not a judge*. And, if you really think you've been that wronged and your case is that solid, the place to be is not in traffic school, it's *in front of a judge*—at the time and place noted, by the way, on your ticket.

Now the Pissed-Off Guy, demonstrating his story, complete with hand movements (including the finger quotes around "running the red"), waited for the instructor's verdict, completely unaware that if everybody in the class—despite the great temptation that it is to testify in front of strangers—held their "I Was Wronged" tale of woe and unjustice, we'd get out of class about ten minutes after roll call was taken and we went over what red, yellow, and green mean. But no, no, no, the Pissed-Off Guy needed validation that he'd been screwed twice, setting the stage for about sixty other stories to be told.

"I was in the intersection already on the yellow," he explained again. "So I don't see why I'm here."

Thankfully, the instructor, skilled at handling such meanderings, looked at the Pissed-Off Guy and said merely, "Well, that's too bad. This lady over here"—and then he winked as he pointed to a woman in the third row—"put all six of her kids in her van and drove to McDonald's and she got a ticket! Why'd she get a ticket? She forgot that she drank a fifth of vodka that morning—didn't you?"

The lady laughed.

From the second row, Grandpa Munster snored, the only indication that he was still alive, since his eyebrows hung over his eyes like dead vines.

"Let's talk about driving under the influence, because in this class we're going to learn how to DRIVE TO SURVIVE!" he continued.

"Give me those keys!!" Grandpa Munster called as he woke with a start.

For the rest of that morning, we learned about how much liquor it actually takes to blow an "impaired" score on the Breathalyzer, which was, frighteningly, very little—according to my state law if you kiss a person who's just had a beer, you're too drunk to drive. One glass of wine is enough to drag an average-sized woman to the pokey and assign her a public defender, and the first thing that came to my mind was that after this class was over, I was going to clean out the closest Krispy Kreme and devour it all in one sitting if that's the way the game is played. That's right, if an average-sized woman can't drink one glass of wine with dinner without becoming a felon on the way home, I don't even know what the point of living is, so there was no other choice but to expand myself to the size of a tract home. To make matters worse, the instructor went on to explain how drinking coffee, downing a cup of Listerine, or enjoying a refreshing mint before the cop gets to the driver's-side window will not help lessen that score, and that all of those things had just been taking up unnecessary room under my car seat for more than a decade. The cherry on the cake was that we learned that by refusing the Breathalyzer test, the suspected drunk person not only gets a one-year suspended license but an automatic DUI as well.

A man in the back row raised his hand.

"That's not exactly true," he said. "I'm a prosecutor in Kingman, and that's not the law."

"Oh, thank God," I mumbled to myself. "If it's anything short of a carafe, I'm getting the surgery to get Carnie Wilson's leftover stomach implanted."

"It is a suspended license," the prosecutor said. "But it's not an automatic DUI."

"What's the law on left-hand turns and red lights?" the Pissed-Off Guy called from across the room.

"My boyfriend got a DUI, and when we went to court this week they lost the paperwork!" Paris Hilton blurted out from the next to last row. "They won't find it, will they? He can't go to prison, he can't! I need to use my phone!"

"Shhh, shhhh," her friend said, putting her arm around her to comfort the crying girl as the guy who sat behind them stared down their ass cracks.

"Did you know that passing in a lane can KILL you? Ask this lady," the instructor said as he pointed to a woman in the back and gave another wink. "She was eating a Big Mac, reading a book, and watching her soap opera while doing eighty on the freeway and trying to pass an RV! We're going to learn how to DRIVE TO SURVIVE!"

"That's *my* hard-boiled egg!" Grandpa Munster said as he jolted awake.

After we learned that you can get a $400 ticket just by using the HOV lane to pass someone if you are the lone passenger in your car, a cluster of horrified gasps escaped from the class as if the O.J. verdict had come in all over again. People were still shaking their heads as we moved on to a film narrated by a self-described "Anti-Terrorism Driving Expert" who explained that the danger and peril out there on the roads was equal to the danger you would experience from terrorism, mainly because of road rage and potholes.

"The driver coming toward you may be the closest thing you ever experience to a terrorist attack," the narrator warned, although I have to admit I failed to see the correlation between someone flipping me off and, say, the bus I'm on blowing up.

Then the film centered on a charred telephone pole that a teenager had driven into, and then staged interviews with the boy's friends and family at the crash site, all with the blackened pole somewhere in the background. Oddly enough, no potholes in the general vicinity were charged with or even suspected of operating on orders from an Axis of Evil country.

Finally, it was time for lunch and Paris Hilton pulled herself together enough to call her boyfriend and assure him the paperwork was "probably pretty lost," the oil drum ran down the stairs to get the money order, and the Pissed-Off Guy was complaining that he couldn't believe we only had forty minutes for lunch, I'm assuming because that was only long enough to squeeze in a lap dance or two at the nearest skanky strip joint.

Grandpa Munster was still sleeping in his chair when I left.

He was still there when I came back, although his *Drive to Survive* workbook had slid to the floor.

I took my seat, as did everyone else, and as soon as the instructor told us to turn to a certain page number, he looked up and walked toward me.

"Speaking of speeding, I saw this lady at lunchtime," the instructor said as he pointed at me and winked, "and she must have been hungry because she was burning rubber in her red-hot Camaro!"

I gasped. I had been utterly anonymous up until this point, I hadn't opened my mouth once. I was just another traffic offender in another driving class, trying to make it through the day. And now, my anonymous time was up. Laurie the Annoyed had been awakened. I was going to have to say something, otherwise risk the chance of being branded as "that white-trash Camaro girl who was too fat to be on crystal meth."

"No, I wasn't," I said blankly.

"Yes, you were!" the instructor said. "Yes, you were! I saw you, squealing your tires in your red Camaro!"

"It wasn't me," I protested, thinking, Why couldn't I have been the drunk mom driving her kids to McDonald's? Why, out of all these people, out of all the cars in the world, did you have to pair me with a RED Camaro and make me pretend to violate my staunchest Cardinal Rule? I'd much rather be the drunk mom than a chick in a tube top, cowboy hat, and white-leather ankle boots.

"You can say I was driving a Pacer, you can say I was driving a Gremlin, you can even say I was driving an El Camino, but I will not cop to driving a Camaro. I'm sorry," I explained. "I can't do it. I've only been in a Camaro once, and it was against my will. And better judgment."

The instructor jumped right back in. "Okay, you were driving a . . . Firebird!" he finished.

"Please pick something else!" I insisted. "Anything else! I will even drive a Geo for you, or a minivan. We'll compromise! How about a Mazda?"

"Okay, fine, a Mazda," he said drolly. "And boy, did you burn some rubber as you tore through that red light! Let's learn how to DRIVE TO SURVIVE!"

"I was hoping we'd get to this part," the Pissed-Off Guy said, suddenly invigorated.

Paris Hilton sighed and then pretended to strangle herself.

We spent the next two minutes talking about red lights, when it's considered running a red light and when it's considered a yellow. We spent the next eighteen minutes after that reenacting the Pissed-Off Guy's traffic incident in a diagram he forced the instructor to draw on the board. They went over the scenario again and again, like it was a choreographed football move in the last minutes of the Super Bowl, an eraser symbolizing the Pissed-Off Guy's 4 x 4, with dry-erase markers and the instructor's wallet portraying other vital roles in the *Mystery of the Left-Hand Turn* play.

Finally, after the instructor, who, by the way, played the Evil Cop role because Harvey Keitel wasn't available, completed the scene for the sixth time, and to the Pissed-Off Guy's satisfaction, even he was worn down.

"Can we just say that it's weird you got the second ticket?" the instructor begged. "Class is almost over and we'll have to stay longer to finish."

"You were wronged!" a man called out from behind me.

"You should sue the cop that gave you the second ticket!" another man yelled.

"You should have given the COP the ticket," the drunk mother joined in.

"That's what I thought!" the Pissed-Off Guy, now known as the Pissed-Off Guy Was Right, said gleefully. "That's what I thought! Thank you. Thank you!"

"Okay, let's move on. I heard they got a guy going one-seventeen on the freeway last week, and that was you, wasn't it, cutting all sorts of people off?" the instuctor interrupted and pointed to Grandpa Munster, who still didn't wake up. "Let's learn to DRIVE—"

"—TO SURVIVE!" the class, minus Grandpa Munster, finished.

After we learned why speeding was bad unless you wanted your family and friends to star in a driver's-ed movie about your death and be questioned in front of the charred telephone pole that decapitated you, the instructor passed out evaluation forms.

"When I went to go get my money order at lunch, I was almost run off the road! The driver in front of me OBVIOUSLY DID NOT use the three-second-cushion-for-safe-following rule that we just learned about! Now, I drive a semi, and the last thing you want to do is cut me off and make me slam on my brakes! Because I can't!"

"You drive a semi?" a guy asked from a couple of rows over.

"Do you live in there?" another man asked.

"Where do you sleep?" a girl behind me asked.

The oil barrel lit up like an orphan who had just found a family with a pretty new mommy and went into great detail about the laws of entering and exiting a truck through the passenger side because her vehicle was her legal home in which she could get drunk.

Everyone was very impressed.

"I pull a horse trailer," a woman behind the oil barrel commented, to which no one said anything.

"On my lunch break, I saw a man making a right-hand turn from the far lane," another woman said. "And he was speeding the whole time before that even happened."

Then, from the middle row, there was some stirring, a head raised, a throat cleared, and Grandpa Munster came out of his coma just as the evaluations were being passed down his aisle and we were ready to call the coroner.

"An evaluation?" he said. "I have something to evaluate! Evaluate why there's a minimum speed limit. Why is there a minimum speed limit? It's not posted, but I learned that one the hard way. And where is the comment section? I don't like these chairs *at all*. Something needs to be done about these chairs."

"Is there a number to call to report bad drivers?" someone else asked. "Because I would like to have it if you know it."

"I am still amazed at the HOV-lane rules," another lady said.

"I think a lot of people could use this class," the Pissed-Off Guy Was Right said. "Very informative."

"Everyone should take this class," the truck driver said. "But you should really take checks."

It was like being in traffic school had reawakened something in every sucky driver in the class. It was as if a reckoning took place: We had accepted the Drive to Survive greater force as our road-time scripture, our driving-school teacher its apostle, and the next time we would be behind the wheel we'd be born-again drivers. I was amazed at my classmates; they buzzed amongst one another with driving-atrocity stories—"Once I saw a man make a right turn from a left-hand lane. I did! It's true!" or "Just the other day, I saw a woman zipping along in the HOV lane *completely* alone, and it was eight fifty-seven! A.M.! Oh, if I only knew then what I know now, or had that bad-driver number to call and report her!"

It was contagious. It was like a cult, or a week at church camp deep in the woods where they show your very malleable and im-pressionable brain a disturbing film about bar codes and a world in which the proper half simply evaporates and the rest of the planet either gets crucified on streetlights or has to join forces with Darth Vader, and then they offer to sell you a "Child of God" Ziggy T-shirt, and should you decline, there's the obligatory look from all those Ziggys around you that says, "Get ready for the nails, then. You've basically asked for it." Everyone had a horror story of someone else's poor driving skills, and before I knew it, there was a girl recounting how every week when she had com-muted back and forth to Tucson, she would see people reading at the wheel, which was bad enough, but books on tape *were readily and widely available at the time*! I rolled my eyes until I realized I was standing up, shaking my right fist in the air, and that it was me re-counting.

"Sing it, sister!" someone else shouted from a back row.

"We hear you, Red Camaro Lady, we hear you!" someone else seconded.

"These chairs are too hard," Grandpa Munster contributed again. "My whole body is asleep and I'm stuck in this position."

"Is class over?" Paris Hilton called. "I have to make a phone call."

On the way out of the parking lot, the cars drove slowly, in single file, everyone used their blinker, and everyone waited a second or two at the stop sign, except for Grandpa Munster, who stayed there until he woke up again.

Everybody on the way home, I bet, was just driving and surviving.

But It Won't Fit Up My Nose

My husband looked at me like I had a kilo of cocaine in my hand instead of a bag from a bookstore.

"Don't you dare bring that thing in this house," he said, blocking the front door so I couldn't get in. "We simply cannot go on living like this! You know the rules!"

Indeed I did.

"It's only one. It's just one little book," I coaxed, as he huffed, dropped his arm, and permitted me inside.

Unfortunately, I married a book guy. My ideal plan was to marry a tool guy, not only so that sticky windows and leaky faucets would be remedied without paying for a house call, but that I might also get a redwood deck out of the deal. However, the tool guy I could have picked up an option on smelled a lot like Sears, and when the book guy came along, he smelled like shaving cream and Downy. Thus, not only did we get married, but two book collections collided and, as a result, we were book bound. I shoved books in drawers, in the china cupboard, in the pantry, and, honestly, if you think John Nash was impressive, you should take a peek at the mathematically impossible stacking configurations I executed in order to get the most space out of our bookshelves. Oriental rugs have never been woven with such complexities.

As time passed, our book collection took on the proportions of free-range feral cats that multiply into six more as soon as two of them touch each other. It came down to this: Either hire a Sherpa to help us navigate around the tall towers of books in our house, dump some of the books, or dump the marriage (I had, admittedly, started rethinking the tool-guy thing anyway when new blinds needed to be installed and flushing the toilet evoked a sound in our pipes very similar to a choir of Benedictine monks).

In order to try and solve the problem, each of us went through our respective libraries and culled every book we believed we could part with, hauled them all to a used-book store, where we traded them for store credit, and each returned with a box of new books.

Clearly, we needed a plan, preferably an effective one, because our current plan was the equivalent of trying to lose weight by eating a package of reduced-fat Oreos at every meal.

"I say we make a book box," my husband, the book guy, said, "and the rule is that if you don't absolutely love a book after you've read it, you have to put it in the box and when it's full we'll donate it to charity."

"Perfect! And how about," I said as my big fat idea met my big fat mouth, "every time we get a new book, we have to give one away?"

And so the Rules were born, and I thought it was a fabulous idea until the day came when my giveaway stash—which included all of the books I had never returned to the library in high school, botany and statistics textbooks from college, books with puffy, embossed covers, and Rosie O'Donnell biographies my mother ("All I'm saying is that you'd get a lot farther in life if you were as nice as Rosie, that's all I'm saying") insists on giving me as gifts—was depleted.

I had to get creative, and, admittedly, sneaky. I quietly opened the creaky door to my office closet and slipped a new paperback behind rolls of gift wrap and packing peanuts. Months passed, seasons changed. My one hidden book had expanded to a whole shelf, my awful terrible secret—that is, until the black, horrible day my husband ran out of staples. As I stood in the kitchen, I heard the creaky door of deceit open, a rustling of paper, a gasp, and then silence.

My husband came into the kitchen, where I was frozen.

"How will I ever be able to trust you with another book again?" he said, not even able to look me in the eye. "You could be holding the TV Guide, and now, I'll wonder. I'll *always wonder*."

"I didn't plan for this to happen," I said looking away, not able to look at his eyes not looking at me. "I didn't want you to find out this way."

"The whole time," he said sadly, "the book box was a lie."

"The book box was a lie," I whispered, nodding slowly. "Except that we have two copies of *Lolita*, so I gave yours to the box. Mine had a cooler cover."

His eyes suddenly met mine in an icy, hard stare. "MY *Lolita*?" he questioned harshly. "My Lo-Lee-Ta?"

The next day, feeling infinitely guilty for giving away his copy, even if the girl on his cover looked a bit tartish and wasn't even remotely as cute as the girl on my cover, I went to the bookstore and bought him a new one. I came home, and after visiting my office closet, I slipped into my husband's office quietly as he watched TV in the next room. I placed the new, unsoiled, perfect new *Lolita* on his keyboard. As I opened the door to leave, it abruptly stopped three-quarters of the way, blocked, I saw, by several tall, teetering stacks of books, shiny new books and some used, none of which I had ever seen before.

The book box was indeed a lie.

I smiled to myself.

I'm awfully glad they're not tools, I thought.

Booty Call

"I want to go home," Jamie said as she looked at me and pouted. "I'm having a rotten time here. Let's just go. We clearly don't belong!"

I was stunned. We had been in San Francisco only for a matter of minutes—only long enough to check into our hotel room—and already she wanted to leave.

"But we come here every year for our birthdays and we always have a great time," I argued. "Just relax. We'll get settled and then head over to get a cookie from the French bakery around the corner."

"I don't want to go anywhere," Jamie asserted. "I'm too embarrassed. Didn't you see as we drove up that every single woman in San Francisco had amazing black leather boots on? Every single one, except two: you and me. We're going to stand out like sore thumbs. Everyone will know we're tourists and the street people will hit us up for money even more."

I laughed. "You're upset because we don't have black boots? You're forgetting that the French bakery isn't the only reason we stay in this hotel. It's also because of the great Indian food joint around the corner, the incredible breakfast place down the street, the free croissants and doughnuts in the morning by the coffee machine, *and*," I said, pointing out the window, "the largest designer shoe warehouse in all of San Francisco, proudly boasting three floors of nothing but discount high-end footwear, visible right now through that window."

"Oh my God," Jamie gasped as she covered her mouth. "Look! I see boots! Rows and rows of nothing but black boots! If there was a sign that said 'Free!' or even 'Seventy-five Percent Off Our Already Incredibly Low Prices' I would think we had died and maybe weren't such selfish, shallow people after all!"

"I know," I said, nodding my head and looking across the street. "Cheap, cool shoes. That's as close to heaven as you can get. Let's go. My buzz from the drinks on the plane is wearing off, and if there's anything I loathe more than religion and taxes, it's another woman touching the shoes that I want."

As we entered the store, both Jamie and I gasped with amazement, overwhelmed by the vast variety of choices. There were black boots everywhere, lined up along every top shelf, like spires on a castle. We dove in hungrily, tossing our purses aside and grabbing every long boot box in our size. Jamie, the more coordinated of the two of us, was the first to kick off her sneakers and slide her foot into a glorious, shiny tall boot. I was right behind her, whipping off a shoe and getting ready to ram my foot into a pair of my own when I heard a sharp cry and realized it was coming from my friend.

"I can't get it up!" she cried. "I can't get this zipper up! It won't fit! This boot won't fit!"

"Well, it must be broken," I said, eager to see myself walking around in my own pair of black San Francisco native boots. "Try the other one."

"I did!" Jamie shot back. "I can't get that one up, either!"

"Then get the next size up," I replied, as I pulled the zipper on my pair of boots, which worked absolutely, perfectly, fabulously fine until it reached the middle of my leg.

"It's not my foot that doesn't fit," Jamie whispered harshly. "It's . . . my . . . *calf!*"

"You mean it's *our calves*," I informed her while my fingers were turning purple with bruises and blood clots trying to force the boot zipper over the state fair–winning watermelon that had apparently seeded and grown in between my knee and ankle.

I turned to look at Jamie, who was staring at me with her mouth hanging open all the way to the top of her unzipped boots.

"Fatty calves," we whispered to each other. "Calf bloat!"

We couldn't believe it. When had this happened? *How* had it happened? How do you just wake up one day and find your last flattering feature has deserted you like a guy who freaks out the first time you bring a stick of your deodorant to his house? I suppose, however, that there were signs. Signs such as the time I was trying to tie my shoe and my very own fat tube bucked backward with a reverse roll into my abdomen and completely bit me; signs such as the instant that I looked in the mirror and saw Tipper Gore's neck underneath my head; signs such as our only party motto was "If you lose me, look for the cheese platter"; or the sign of how I pledged my loyalty to the Awesome Blossom despite the fact that I received, and read, the mass e-mail that said it contained 300 grams of fat. Looking back, I suppose it was only a matter of time before the trickle-down theory was applied to the excess of my paunch and began to distribute itself evenly to my few remaining skinny parts, like my knuckles, earlobes, and now, apparently, my calves.

Indeed, the realization that fatty calves had assumed resident status on our legs was a chilling moment and in hindsight ranked in third place in my list of Horrifying Moments of Truth in my life, preceded only by:

The Second Most Horrifying Moment of Truth, 11:53 P.M., October 5, 1999: Previously, I could have sworn that every kernel of the

Dripping with Butter at the Movies Microwave Popcorn that I was addicted to had been individually kissed by butter angels had I not once accidentally opened a prepopped packet of butter-marinated popcorn and seen the horror inside for myself. There, lying quietly inside the bag, was an orange gelatinous puddle the color of sinister toxic waste and the consistency of a bar of Irish Spring. It looked as if someone had melted, then solidified, Ronald McDonald and squirted him into bags of kernels. It was vile. It was unnatural. It was definitely cancer. Don't get me wrong, it tasted great when the popping was all said and done, but it was kind of like unexpectedly seeing your mom naked. It was the brand of truth you shouldn't even attempt to handle yourself without the aid of a skilled professional, and I firmly believe that stuff should be renamed "At the Movies in Chernobyl" Microwave Popcorn.

and

The First and Most Paramount Horrifying Moment of Truth, 10:47 A.M., May 2, 1978: I permitted Kay, a stoner chick and the only person who would talk to me in Beginning Choir at Shea Middle School, to look into my eighth-grade clutch purse for a stick of gum because her breath reeked of the joint she had just consumed by herself. I watched helplessly as her hand emerged from my purse, not with a stick of gum, but with the toothbrush that I had to carry because of my braces, which now had the exposed strip of a maxi pad stuck to it. With the handle of the toothbrush in her hand, she raised it up above her head and proceeded to run around the classroom like it was an American flag as she chanted, "Whorie Laurie! Whorie Laurie!"

And now, a new, amazing prolific achievement of my life rolled in as Fatty Calf Syndrome, possibly bumping the Chernobyl popcorn incident.

"What can we do about our enormous bulging calves?" I asked

Jamie in a panic. "A calf-reduction procedure? Deaugmentation? Leg liposuction? Little rubber fat suits from the knee down? How do I put my calves on a diet? What do we do? *What do we do?!!!*"

"What we're going to do," Jamie said, leaning in and furrowing her brow in a definite badge of determination, "is find boots to fit our freakishly large Laura Bush legs. We're in San Francisco, the capital of the world for men, with big men legs, who live to shop for and wear ladies' clothing. There's bound to be a transvestite store somewhere within five square miles that sells boots that our basketball calves can fit into!"

So we embarked on our hunt for the entire rest of the day, scouting out any store windows displaying rubber dresses, clothing with an inordinate amount of sequins, and any Wonder Woman outfits or memorabilia whatsoever. But after we hit eight shoe stores with not one pair that would fit us and one she-male boutique that only carried slippers that were the size of pontoon boats alluringly adorned with pink feathers, we still came up empty-calved, with the exception of a pair of very firm and perky attachable breast forms in case I ever have to start dating again.

I was about to give up when a man named Destiny who had thinner legs and nicer cheekbones than we did overheard our plight at Uncanny Tranny and directed us to a place he said could probably help us.

"I don't know if I can withstand the humiliation of another store," I whined. "Frankly, I think I'd rather play with generic whiskey and a bunch of knives."

"One last store," Jamie gasped as we tried to make it up another steep San Francisco hill. "If we don't succeed this time, I promise we can go back to the hotel room and lie down until our calves atrophy and our bodies eventually absorb them."

"How can I help you?" the cordial shoe man said as soon as we entered the store.

"Someone took half my ass and stuck it under my knee," Jamie said, breathing heavily and pointing to her stout, engorged calf. "And I am not going back out there until I can fit a boot around them."

"And I apparently have Christina Ricci's blow-pop head emerging from behind either of my shins," I added, pointing to my leg loaves. "Oh my God. Either those are cellulite potholes or they're forming sockets for eyes!"

"This happens a lot," the jolly shoe man said as he emitted a deep, heavy sigh and shook his head. "Active ladies like yourselves often pay a price for their athletic lifestyles, and I'm afraid this is one of the tolls. Boot manufacturers make boots sized for models—but models don't walk, they have drivers! They're lazy skinny people! It's a horrible side effect of having such a finely sculptured calf, as opposed to a flat, flappy supermodel one."

"You are so right!" Jamie gushed. "Who wants a pancake for a calf when you can have a Cinnabon? This calf shows the dedication to my sport, even if I really haven't considered taking one up yet!"

"I have a hobby," I volunteered meekly. "It's chicken fried steak."

"I have just the boots for you!" he said as he snapped his fingers and disappeared into the back room.

Now, true, he was using the term "athletic" as loosely as the skin that's gathered like drapes around Elizabeth Taylor's head, but frankly, I didn't care. If he wanted to pretend that our calves were well developed rather than identify them as the lumps of cellulite and homes to a lifetime of Hostess Ding Dong toxic waste deposits that they really were, I was totally into it. He had earned his commission from me, and if there was any way he was willing to point out the firmness of my rock-in-a-sock boobs, I'd kick in another five bucks as well.

Honestly, I don't know what I expected from a man who would lie straight to my double chin and John Goodman neck and tell me that I looked "athletic," but I did expect something more than what I saw when he opened the two boxes of boots and presented us with his fat-calf bounty.

Jamie was the first to speak. "Wow," she said slowly and quietly. "Are those . . . pirate boots?"

"Well, let's just say they have a swarthy influence to them," the exuberant shoe man glowed. "Aren't they wonderful?"

"Sure, if I had some pieces of eight and a hook hand to go with them," I said, staring at the big silver buckle and the way they folded over the top.

"And perhaps a parrot and a peg leg," Jamie added as she picked up one of the boots from her box and began to try it on.

"These are the only boots you have?" I asked.

The friendly shoe man nodded. "And these are the last two pairs in your size," he added.

"I'll take them," Jamie said as she walked around the store with them, looking as if she was about to pillage a schooner.

"Oh, all right, I'll take them, too," I said, but only after I was sure they could swallow and digest my bulbous leg mushrooms. "At least if I know that when I'm short on money, I can either get hooked up at the Pirates of the Caribbean or a community theater production of *Peter Pan*."

As the friendly shoe man was swiping our Visas and thanking God Almighty that he had finally unloaded inventory that had sat on his shelf since Adam Ant still had a career, I turned to my friend, Captain Ahab.

"We're going to look like assholes, you know," I said.

"I know," she answered. "But at least we'll look like *native* assholes. Ahoy, matey."

Web M.D.

"Oh, look at those fat little sausage ankles," my Nana said to me last week. "Those look like clown feet! I've only seen ankles like that one time before, and that was on your Aunt Judy. Two days later she was lying in a casket and wearing green eye shadow that made her swollen head look like a Granny Smith apple."

I looked down and gasped in horror. My ankles suddenly had the circumference of a Goodyear tire that hadn't exploded yet, and were as round and full as a python that had just finished eating a native. Holy shit, first the cantaloupe calves and now this, I thought mournfully as I sighed. They were the last segments of my body where I could actually still see my bones.

My sisters recoiled in disgust.

"Whoa," my sister said. "Did your husband leave you yet?"

"Wow, there goes your last flattering feature," my other sister said.

"Your aunt's heart failed and then exploded so hard it nearly shot out of her nose," Nana continued. "You should go to the doctor."

I didn't want to go to the doctor. Everyone there knows how much I weigh, they won't take my checks, but they do take secret notes about me that I'm not allowed to see and then read them into a tape recorder. I wouldn't tolerate that on any other social occasion, particularly one when I'm wearing nothing but a paper-towel poncho, so in my book, those experiences are ones that need to be regulated and limited, much like court appearances.

So instead, when I got home I turned to my trusty computer. A search on "swollen ankles" pointed me to several Web medical sites that were only too anxious to tell folks how grave their disease was and, comparatively speaking, how long you had before a head of broccoli would outlive you.

The first indication that the situation warranted some concern was that a list of possible swollen ankle–related illnesses took longer to download than it did for me to meet my husband for the first time and get him drunk enough to think I was pretty.

It was not good news.

Like a disease buffet, it offered me a variety of misfortunes to choose from. The first on the list was congestive heart failure, along with a variety of symptoms.

"Weight gain (unintentional)," the first one read, and I nodded.

"That has my name written on it," I said aloud. "I certainly didn't put 'ass the size of a sleeper sofa' on my Christmas list last year, but I sure got it anyway."

"Shortness of breath, especially with activity and cough," the list continued.

"SEE?" I sighed. "I *knew* it wasn't because I smoked!"

"Decreased concentration, addiction to chocolate Twizzlers, and swelling of feet and ankles," the list concluded.

Check, check, check, I tallied. When I compiled my score and read the results, the Web doctor informed me that I had approximately twelve minutes to shave my most embarrassing spots and then put on clean underwear, because did I really want paramedics to see me that way? Contrary to popular opinion, they *are* horrified by the grotesque and will make fun of you when you slip into unconsciousness.

And that wasn't all. My soggy, deformed heart was the smallest of my problems, at least for my last seven minutes of life. Odds were also good to excellent that I was host to diabetes, lupus, tuberculosis, liver failure, circulatory distress, kidney failure, and also that my brain was being eaten away in large bites by gonorrhea.

I quickly called my regular doctor, who said to come to his office immediately.

"Hurry," I said to him as I jumped up on his examination table and my paper dress twirled about me like the blades of a windmill. "My heart is going to shoot out my nose any minute now. That is, unless my liver turns to dust, I suffocate in my own fluids, or the very last bit of my brain is smeared on a cracker and gobbled up by VD."

"Let's take a look," he said, holding my feet.

"You're going to amputate because of the diabetes, aren't you?" I said, shaking my head. "Oh God. Maybe it won't be so bad, you know? I'd always have a seat at the movie theater, I'd save a ton on shoes, and maybe I could even win an Olympic medal in the 75-meter roll. Instead of a Wheaties box, they could put my face on a box of syringes."

"Did someone give you a medical encyclopedia?" he asked curiously. "How did you come up with all of these diseases?"

"The www.diseaseroulette.com and www.maladyexpress.net," I said simply. "I have the symptoms of all of them."

He sighed. "What you have is the Village Idiot Home Diagnosis Syndrome. Don't ever look up stuff on medical sites again! It's the heat of the summer that's made your feet freak-show size."

"So I'm just FAT," I said blankly.

"There's really no happy answer to that," he said, although I was nearly positive from his hand motions that he wrote "F-A-T" on my chart, in addition to the words "last flattering feature."

Terror and Death at the
Black House

The screaming started the moment I walked into my mother's house to bring Easter baskets for my nephews.

It was the familiar chorus of all the sounds regularly heard when opening the door to my mother's house: my eight-year-old nephew, Nicholas, crying; my four-year-old nephew, David, screaming; the TV blaring; and somewhere, in the background, my mother yelling for everyone to knock it off.

As soon as Nicholas was born, my mother swore she'd rather see her daughters become Jehovah's Witnesses or pole dancers before she saw her first grandchild in daycare when my sister went back to work. I don't think it was orignally the idea of daycare that didn't sit well with her but the fact that there, in a bassinet, was a fresh slate, a lump of clay that could be worked on and molded into the perfect child who had eluded her the first time around with her own daughters. A kid whom she could take to church, a kid who would give up something for Lent and eagerly abide by it, a kid who couldn't wait to eat fish on Fridays and who would actually keep the smudge on his forehead on Ash Wednesday and not pretend to have a sweaty forehead and "accidentally" wipe it off when she returned them to school, unlike her own kids.

"That's Jesus on your head!" she would bellow from the driver's seat of the station wagon as we got out and went back to school as all the kids on the playground stopped and stared as three girls with filthy faces got out of the screaming lady's car. "God will see it if you wipe it off! If you wipe it off, the Devil wins! Don't you dare wipe it off, I wrote all of you excuses for PE today. And no running at recess! No sweating!"

"If that kid needs even one DAY of psychotherapy," I told my mother when it was decided that the baby would stay with her, "I'm going to sue you, Mom."

The mother of my childhood was not the kind of mother who was prone to messing around, particularly when it came to discipline. If you didn't listen to her commands and obey the first time around, chances were good to excellent that you were going to quickly be acquainted with her shoe, which did double duty, serving not only as inexpensive footwear but as a flyswatter, battering ram, and paddle, or with her fingers, which could substitute for a vise grip and should have been patented by Black & Decker. Her favorite phrase was not "Wait till your father comes home" but "When your father comes home this will be a quiet house, because if you don't behave, *right now*, I'm calling The Lady and taking you to the orphanage!"

I was already a nervous kid to begin with, I really didn't need any assistance in the drama department, such as hearing threats that I would be a free agent at four years old. One day in kindergarten, I forgot my lunch and threw up on my teacher's shoes. The same year, our bus was in a minor fender bender, and, being the spaz that I am, I was the only one who got hurt: I ended up with a black eye and believed I had swallowed a tooth. So I threw up. As I got off the bus that day, I ran to my pregnant mother and wrapped my arms around her legs in search of comfort. My mother, however, despite my sobs and throw-up-splattered dress, wrenched me off of her with those Black & Decker claws and pushed me away harshly. That's when I discovered that not only wasn't she my mother, just some random pregnant lady, but it wasn't even my stop. After eating flounder every Friday as every good Catholic toddler does to prevent my Downy-fresh soul from spinning in purgatory, I finally asked my mother if I could eat something else, and when she refused, I staged a Vomit Revolution, and the battlefield where I attacked was the dining room table. That, I am proud to say, is a war I won.

Now, though I doubt she got the "orphanage" behavior-modification technique out of Dr. Spock's Baby Basics, it pretty much did the trick most of the time, especially after she took me to see the film version of Oliver Twist and I spent the next significant portion of my life terrified that I would wake up one day and my Count Chocula would be replaced with gruel, my clothes would begin to unravel and turn brown, and I'd have to share a bed with a girl who smelled, although singing and dancing in a synchronized group looked like fun and might give me a chance to show off my talents at leaping and acting plucky.

Not that I could blame her; my mother, much like every other mother of the time, was under thirty with three kids, which even I consider an unfortunate situation that should require some sort of reparations for a stolen youth. Frankly, if at twenty-five, I was driving a station wagon, boiling hot dogs for dinner three nights out of the week, changing diapers and helping people with their homework instead of hanging out with my friends until four A.M., sleeping until noon, and taking off for an impromptu road trip on occasion, I'd be hitting people with my shoes and pinching them at random, too.

But the grandmother of my nephews was different from the mother I knew.

My nephews' grandmother bought them McDonald's for a snack when they came home from school, read them books, and played with them. She took them to their gymnastics lessons, their T-ball games, their soccer matches. She bought them toys when they went shopping and let them invite their friends over to swim. I really don't think she had grown more patient, just a whole lot more tired, but her shoes stayed on her feet, mainly because it hurt to bend over and untie them and she had begun to have her Carmela Soprano nails professionally done, so pinching in any situation except for self-defense was nothing short of throwing good money right out the window.

My mother, it turned out, was the cool grandma.

That is, until the day I opened the door and the screams erupted as the kids started fighting over a toy car. I heard my mother yell from an upstairs bedroom, "Boys! You'd better behave or I'm calling The Lady!"

A chill went up my spine, and I suddenly had the urge to grab a wooden bowl and spin around the living room, singing the chorus of "Food, Glorious Food."

And then I remembered the day my mother made good on her threats and took me to the Black House.

I am four.

It's a cold February day in New York. My mother has me all bundled up outside, and my whole family gets into the car, even my Nana and Pop Pop. I wonder where we are all going, but no one is saying anything.

Now, this is where the story gets weird. My dad parks the car, we all get out and walk up to a house I swear was painted black. I wasn't really on my guard at this point, it was far too early. There were no signs, I like to tell myself, there was no way to know what lay just a couple of minutes ahead for me; I probably had just had a snack, my black eye was almost healed, and I was forever excused from seafood of all types. Things were looking up.

Until we go into the Black House and sit on a wooden bench at the bottom of the stairs. I can't figure out what's going on until I realize my sister is not with us. And then it hits me.

I am at The Orphanage. My mother was not bullshitting me. I

am being put up for adoption because I am the Throw-Up Girl. No one wants a kid who throws up on a teacher. No one wants a kid who throws up on a bus and then can't even recognize her own mother. No one wants a kid who throws up all over Friday's Catholic Family Fun Fish Fry.

No one.

Panic shoots ice through my veins and I am one scared little kid. I want to throw up but I pretty much figure I should probably not move on that need until later, considering the circumstances. I decide to go for the softest, easiest target in the group, my Nana.

"Nana, I'll be good, please, I promise," I beg. "I promise I'll be good, I don't want to go."

My poor, kind Nana smiles and pats me on the head. "That's nice, sweetheart," she says. "Now just sit here like a good girl."

Sure, strategy isn't a well-honed skill at the age of four unless you live in Thailand and you and your twin brother are heading your very own guerrilla insurgency, but I'm doing my best. I hit my Pop Pop up next with pleas of behaving and sharing toys and being really, really good. He looks at me with a sad smile and says, "Oh, Laurie, you'll be all right. Everything will be fine."

Before I can move on to my parents and change their minds about surrendering me to a life of brown muslin dresses, bunk beds with dirty sheets, and selling matches to earn a living, something unspeakable happens. From the top of the stairs, a *Nightmare on Elm Street*–caliber scream is emitted, forceful, shrill, obviously from a child—and with my luck the person I'm going to be sleeping under for the next fourteen years.

I listen to the scream in its entirety as everything goes silent around it, my eyes trained on the dark, shadowy top of the stairs. When the sharp, long, horrible, terrified scream finally ends, there is no movement, there is no sound but the fresh memory of it repeating in my head as if on a loop.

Despite the chances, things have just gotten worse.

I am not at the children's orphanage, I slowly understand.

But I *am* at the children's slaughterhouse.

Before I know it, a nurse has me by the arm and is attempting to lead me up the stairs, and I know enough to fight, despite the confusion that is swallowing me in big gulps. This must be The Lady my mom's always talking about, I think. I don't get a chance to see my family for the last time, and I don't get a chance to say good-bye, I don't even get the opportunity to offer up eating flounder as a bargaining chip, or at least cleaning up my own vomit. It's just over. I am going to die.

Before I know it, I'm on a table somewhere in the death chamber, there are huge machines all around me and big lights. When the nurse turns around, she's got a mask in her hand, she's coming at me with the mask pointed toward my mouth, saying, "Now breathe deep, Laurie," and she's coming closer and closer and closer and closer, and when she's just inches from me, when she's just this far away, I yell as loud as I can in a battle cry and then punch her right in the neck with all the force I've got. I balled up my little fist and coldcocked her. From there, it took two other nurses and a doctor to hold me down—I was swingin' like a monkey—and then, suddenly, everything went black.

When I wake up, hours later, there is a brand-new Dawn Beauty Pageant doll box at the end of my bed and I can't talk. It takes me a while to figure out that I am back home, and that I must have put up one hell of a fight because I'm not dead. In fact, I was such a good fighter that I even got a present out of the deal.

I try to talk, but nothing comes out and my throat hurts. Those bastards tried to strangle me, I figure, or punched me right back in the neck. But I fought back, and by the looks of it, I beat them!

"DON'T TALK, LAURIE," my mother says, loudly, as if my parents didn't try to have me murdered, just rendered deaf and mute just so I would be a quiet fish eater. "WRITE DOWN WHAT YOU WANT."

She then hands me a pad of paper and a pen, but I just look at her, as if to say, "The only thing I can write is my name and my address in case I am kidnapped, *and you know that*," so I try to draw a glass of Pepsi, kind of just a square with a line across it, because I want something to drink.

"What is that?" my mother says quizzically. "Huh. I don't know what the hell that is. Is that a cracker? Are you hungry? Why would you want a cracker? We don't even have that kind of cracker. I don't buy that kind of cracker. That's not our brand. What about a sandwich? A nice sandwich? Well, why not? It's the same shape!"

Eventually, I have to resort to charades to express that I'm thirsty, and after drinking out of a pretend glass like a mime, my mother finally understands.

"Oh, a drink? You're thirsty?" my mother finally guesses. "Because of your throat? It hurts? Because you had your tonsils out?"

As I've said before, my mother always believed that medical procedures were on a need-to-know basis, though that juicy little nugget of news might better have been delivered before I *began fighting evil child-slayers in a desperate attempt to save my life.*

"What's the big deal?" my mother said twenty years later when I questioned her about why she didn't tell me I was about to have a routine surgical procedure and not executed. "I don't know. What the hell difference does it make now?"

"Well, let's see what the effects something like that could have on a little girl who thought her parents took her to be killed?" I asked. "Tell me if any of this rings a bell: low self-esteem, paranoia, cynicism, not to mention an intense, otherwise unexplainable loathing of charades and Pictionary."

"It's not my fault you have a vivid imagination!" my mother said defensively. "Why would I tell a little girl, 'Get in the car, we're going to have things cut out of your neck with a knife'?"

I don't know, maybe she had a point, but as I gave the Easter baskets to my nephews over thirty years later, I couldn't help but shake my head.

"Nicholas," I said as I presented my older nephew with the basket. "Want some chocolate?"

"Nah," he said, looking up at me with his huge brown eyes. "I gave it up for Lent. Grandma said I was getting chubby."

"I want chocolate," David chimed in.

"Okay, here's your basket," I said, handing it over. "But who is the lady Grandma says she's going to call if you don't behave?"

"The daycare lady," Nicholas said. "But I don't want to go to daycare."

"I don't want to go to daycare," David agreed. "Grandma says there's no pool or McDonald's at daycare."

"Well, guess what?" I said. "Grandma is never going to call The Lady. The Lady is never going to come."

"How do you know?" Nicholas asked.

"Because," I explained. "The Lady doesn't exist. There is no lady. The Lady is just in Grandma's head. She has a very vivid imagination."

"Are you sure?" Nicholas said.

"I don't want to go to daycare," David added.

"I'm positive you are never going to daycare," I told them firmly. "And I am positive there's no Lady. There never was and there never will be. But let's practice drawing a glass of Pepsi, just in case."

It's Fun to Stay at the YMCA

I couldn't believe that it had ever come to this.

There I was, standing in the middle of the sports equipment department at Sears about to make a hefty purchase and I was having a little trouble dealing with what I was seeing.

"So this treadmill is eight hundred dollars," I said.

"Plus the two-hundred-dollar warranty," the sales guy, who didn't look old enough to drive a car, let alone make commission, reminded me.

"Plus that," I repeated.

"Plus the delivery charge," the sales guy reminded me again.

"Plus that," I repeated.

"And plus tax," he concluded.

"And plus that," I repeated.

"Brings the total about thirteen hundred, ballpark," he concluded, nodding his head.

"Toss on another thousand or two and I could just get this fat sucked out of my ass in an afternoon!" I said with a tired laugh.

"I know, that's what you said fifteen minutes ago," the sales guy also reminded me.

"It's just a lot," I informed him. "You know."

"I *do* know," he replied. "You said that fifteen minutes ago, too."

"That treadmill is a trip to Europe," I informed him.

"Then maybe you should go to Europe and join the Y for twenty bucks a month," the sales guy replied.

I turned around and looked at him. "For someone who doesn't even have hair on his legs yet, that is just cruel," I said, at which he turned to me and shrugged. "I trusted you!"

You see, I had a choice to make after my doctor took a look at my water-balloon ankles and let it slip about how much I weighed, like I hadn't already heard it in the hallway after "the weigh-in." Now, in this case, if my IQ and my weight were the same, I'd be thrilled, but, frankly, I would have preferred he said something like "Goodness, your husband is a good kisser," or "You know, in high school my son always said you danced like an epileptic. You know that song 'What I Like About You'? He knew you would dance behind him and point at the 'youuuuuu' part. That's why he never turned around." But he didn't. He told me the number, the full number. Unedited, blatant, and nearly pornographic, it had the shock value of a snuff film. That's something I really think I need to take issue with. I mean, guess what? I know what I am. I *know*. There isn't any "XS" dripping off the labels of my clothes, I'm all XL's and L's, although I do have a tendency to employ a defense mechanism and pretend that L is for "Laurie." I'm not buying size fourteen and scratching out the one, convincing only myself that it was mismarked.

In a doctor's office, isn't your care their utmost concern? Isn't your health, both physical *and* mental, their primary goal? Then, Dear God, by all means, what the hell is a SCALE doing there? *The enemy.* That's akin to placing Patty Scevaro, the biggest whore and the meanest girl in high school, right in the hallway to call out as you pass by, "Your ass is a waterbed, Notaro. California King. And you also danced like you were standing in a puddle with a live wire in your hand. We mocked you. Mercilessly." I don't need that kind of pressure at the doctor's office. I know I'm flawed, that's why I'm there *already*. I've thought about running for some sort of political office, my only platform being the abolition of scales in doctor's offices. You wanna get on one at home, fine, but don't force me in front of other people and then announce the results out loud. This is not bingo! This is not the lottery! Nobody wins, there is *no* reason to shout. I believe the very least doctor's offices could do is to give you the option of a blindfold or a dose of Twilite Sleep, just to be kind, or perhaps have a "fun house" scale where it would read a wildly different result depending on where you were standing on it.

Anyway, I had a choice after my doctor busted out with exactly to the ounce how much I weighed. I couldn't just go on a diet; diets plain don't work for me; and, sure, you've heard that before, but in my case it's true. Every time I go on a diet, KFC brings back that popcorn chicken. *Every single time.* I mean, you can even chart it—my going on a diet is to popcorn chicken what the moon is to tides. I'll go as far as to guarantee it, because this has been happening for years. I'll decide to make the plunge, buy all the special food, adapt to the diet of a badger, stifle hunger spasms with rice cakes and grapes, I'll finally lose a pound or two, lay the first brick in the reconstruction of my self-esteem, and POW!!!

Popcorn chicken.

It never fails.

I'm starting to believe that I'm under surveillance, or at least am being tracked like big game. I don't know if KFC franchisees are required to make an official report to the home office of my last visit each time they submit an order for cole slaw and sporks, but *someone* knows. *Someone* is paying attention. There's an intelligence operative out there who sounds the alarm when I haven't been spotted singing to myself in the drive-thru for several weeks. Then the command is given over the loudspeaker at every KFC in the country.

"Red alert! Red alert! All hands report to their frying stations at once!! NOTARO IS M.I.A.!!! BRING BACK THE POPCORN CHICKEN!"

Who can resist popcorn chicken? WHO? I can't! It's POPCORN CHICKEN! Little pieces of chicken dipped in batter and fried to a delicate crisp, little pieces of chicken so tiny they essentially disintegrate in the bubbling oil. All that's left is fried, crunchy bits. A whole box full of fried, crunchy bits. I mean, it's the perfect food.

What I fear most is that KFC hasn't kept this info to themselves. My nutrition information got more mileage than my e-mail address did when it was sold to a pimp with a dirty mouth and relatives in the Internet porn industry. Word is getting out. People start to panic. As if popcorn chicken didn't pose enough of a threat to my inner-thigh Chub Rub, a whole gang of offenders started popping up. You know, it's not like I'm a bastion of will-power or endurance; when I was born, God gave me eight ounces of patience, and by the second day of my life it was *gone*. As a result, if I'm more than a step away from a grape or rice cake when I hear my stomach cry out for help, within seconds I can expect to catch a glimpse of my reflection on the microwave door, gnawing on an empty taco shell or a brick of cheese that I'm holding poised between my two paws like a bear at a campsite.

It's obvious to me that KFC sold my personal information to a bunch of companies that apparently relied on me quite heavily to meet their projected quarterly earnings. Nabisco, for one, immediately stocked store shelves with the new chocolate Oreos a mere fifteen minutes after I was spotted purchasing a bag of carrots one day. It's as if my diet has threatened Nabisco's place in the cookie world, and without my sugar and carbohydrate addiction to count on, they're terrified that Keebler elves may stage a coup and seize the cookie throne.

But that's not all. Once, as I walked out of the grocery store with a week's worth of light yogurt, a massive Kellogg's truck screeched to a halt and started unloading crates of the latest Pop-Tart flavor, chocolate chip, in an attempt to trap me. I also believe that Dreyer's has paid a spy to rewire my cable so that on any channel, I have no other programming choices but Dreamery ice cream commercials.

What choice did I have? I always have to give in. If I stand my ground, soon every magazine that I pick up will be 150 pages of nothing but Milky Way and Twinkie ads. I'm terrified Sonic will send a whole team of waitresses to roller-skate around my front yard until I place an order for a chili cheese dog, a basket of onion rings, and a coconut cream pie shake. I would be pummeled with more temptation than a priest in a USA Network movie. So considering my fat inner-tube ankles, my choices were limited: Dieting was out, and either I could be happy with my new ankles or I could do something about it aside from sticking them with a pin and draining them, risking flood damage in my home. So I did.

I joined the Y. In hindsight, it may not have been the best idea I've ever had, considering my aversion to the nudity of strangers in close proximity to myself. Take, for example, the day that I was quietly washing my hands in the bathroom attached to the locker room when suddenly, out of nowhere, there was a naked lady standing next to me, leaning over the sink to get a closer look in the mirror as she ladled on her mascara. I looked at her for a moment and actually debated saying something, because, really, if you're exerting enough effort to apply makeup, couldn't you just go the extra mile and slap on a bra? Some panties, perhaps? Why was I forced to share breathing space with foreign nipples? Needless to say, the parts of her that should have remained private were entirely all too public, and as she leaned even closer to get a better view of her very own eye, her hinterlands were becoming quite familiar with the sink and soiling it for me forever. From that moment on, every time I spied something black and thin and curly on the floor, even if it was a thread or the plastic stem from a price tag, I'd nod my head and shudder like my skin was about to fall off. I don't care what your views of public nudity are, a random pube encounter is *never* a welcome one, no matter who you are. However, I kept my observations and conclusions to myself, and as long I wasn't forced to use the dirty sink the Naked Mascara Woman had vagina-ized, I was relatively okay.

Other than that, I loved it. I loved the Y. I tried to go every day, and after a while, people even started to know me—like the receptionist, the weight-trainer guy, and all of the other regulars who went the same time I did. They weren't exactly my friends. I mean, we didn't take Gatorade breaks together. But I've learned in my life that if you just keep waving at someone no matter how blankly they look at you, eventually they start to wave back.

Now, my days at the Y started with me putting my stuff in a locker, getting a towel, and going to work on the treadmill. If I was lucky, a trashy talk show would be on the big screen at the front of the gym and I'd get to watch the bottom of the barrel push each other around on a stage as I continually pushed my glasses back up my perspiring nose and trudged along.

One day I decided after I got off the treadmill that I would give the exercise bike a shot. It wasn't a spinning sort of bike, more like the motorcycle Dennis Hopper rode in *Easy Rider*, with long handlebars that arched up in front of the big bucket seat, and holding on to them put my hands up almost level with my ears. True, it wasn't a sexy image, and I rather looked like I was riding a Big Wheel, but listen, I was at the Y and didn't think I'd need to be impressing an audience. Being that the bike was stationed right along a huge glass wall that looked out over the parking lot and not the big-screen TV, I took my glasses off and set them on the console of the bike and started pedaling away. It was hard work, but I was determined to do a full half hour, not just to see if

I could, but also to sweat away my ankles' spare tires, and be-cause an old Polish man with a pelt instead of a back was lying on the weight-lifting bench without a shirt on, getting it nice and gross for everybody else, and the weight-trainer guy was going ballistic.

While I was watching the fight develop—the weight-trainer guy explaining the "shirts-only policy" and the Polish man accusing the weight-trainer guy of accusing him of being dirty, so that the Polish guy invited the weight-trainer guy to smell him to prove that he was not—a line of students had begun to gather on the other side of the glass wall. It was summer, and it made sense to me that there was probably something of a day camp at the Y. The line began to grow, and within a few minutes, there were male students all along the glass wall, laughing, joking, and chiding each other.

That was when several of them noticed me. Which was fine, I can be friendly, I can play along. A group of middle-school-aged boys waved to me. So I waved back. Then they pretended to ride a bike, and, naturally, they placed their hands up by their ears since I was on the retardo bike, which I knew, sure, but it's another thing to have it pointed out to you by a twelve-year-old that you're a spaz. But whatever. Okay, fine, I thought, it's funny, I'm a clown on the circus bike, yeah, okay, I laughed back, made a goofy little look on my face. They laughed.

We were all entertained.

Well, almost all of us.

Apparently, that wasn't enough for one of the boys in this silent little repartee. Making fun of the fat lady with the swollen water-balloon ankles on the dork bike just wasn't enough.

Instead of being satisfied with the little chuckle we had all had, one of the middle schoolers, with his hand, made a gesture that's very common for boys his age, particularly when they're in a bath-room. By themselves.

I'm sure I was visibly shocked, since I gasped and said, then mouthed, "Oh my God, stop that!"

That, however, was the wrong thing to do. Because instead of being embarrassed by his rather graphic hand movements, because even though I didn't have my glasses on, I knew he certainly wasn't churning imaginary butter—instead of being ashamed the way a polite, adult-respecting child on any program on Nickelodeon would be, the kid and his friends laughed even harder, hitting each other on the back like it was a football game and they had just scored a touchdown, and then, through the glass, the nasty one pointed at me.

Fine, I thought to myself, as my knees grazed by my ears on the next revolution, our fun little game is over. You had to turn it dirty. A little clean, lighthearted-old-chunky-lady fun just wasn't enough for you. You had to make it about that. *You had to make it about that.*

Fine, I continued thinking to myself. I'm just going to ride this bike faster, harder, I'm going to turn my anger at you into energy! That might have been a wise move if I'd been born more coordinated, or with any coordination aside from the niblet it takes to chew and swallow, or sit down, because as I was building up to my fury speed—furious enough that I could have powered all of Gilligan's Island—my legs were so consumed with going faster that they couldn't handle communicating to each other about who was doing what, and with the entirety of the line outside watching me, my excited foot freaked out and slipped over the pedal, lurching me forward onto the frame of the bike, and as the pedal whipped around in another rotation, it sliced my big fat calf right up the middle.

This, of course, was better, *far better*, than if that line of boys had been watching an Adam Sandler movie and someone was hit with a turd (of course, I would have laughed at that, too), and one of them laughed so hard he had to pull out an inhaler.

After I saw that, yes, indeed, I was bleeding, I looked up to the glass wall and saw that the severity of my gym-bike injury had not in any way diminished the laughter that was breaking out just on the other side of the wall. In fact, it had perhaps exaggerated the situation, because the boy who was minutes ago pretending to be merely servicing himself was now acting out a complete scene from a porno movie, complete with a partner who was invisible.

Now, I have to admit that I'm not very seasoned about how to respond to situations such as this. I mean, I had never really openly discussed at a cocktail party what the appropriate avenue of response is when an eighth-grader is performing the denoue-ment of *Krakahoa: Bare With Me* for your benefit, but I think it's safe to say that all ability to reason at this point had crashed with me on the stationary bike, and manic instinct took over.

I had had enough. Stationary-bike rage had me in its grasp and I did the only thing I could do.

I flipped him off, that filthy, nasty preteen, I flipped him off. It wasn't the right thing to do, I know that, it's just what bubbled to the surface. It just happened.

That actually did stop him for a minute. I guess he had never had a fat-ankled, sweaty, bleeding lady flip him the finger before. But, then again, he had never met me.

And I understood that all too well when I grabbed my towel, got off the bike, put on my glasses, and realized that I had not really been involved in a hostile, aggressive dialogue of less-than-savory blue sign language with a surly, triple-X-minded eighth-grader, but a surly, triple-X-minded eight-year-old.

I gasped again. I couldn't believe what I had done—now, clearly, with the benefit of corrective lenses—I had become some-thing of a child abuser. I had just flashed an obscene gesture to a second-grader, and sure, that was one of the more mundane things we had seen during this exchange, but still. I was a horrible person. Then, the mere child made the "peace" sign with his fingers, a gesture I took to suggest a mutual truce, so I returned the gesture, slowly and softly, with a sad smile. He had, obviously, realized he had gone too far, and certainly, so had I. I was sorry, too. I was so sorry. At least that's what I was thinking until a moment later when he raised the peace sign up to his mouth and then stuck his tongue through the middle of it, wiggling it around like a serpent.

For a moment I almost flipped him off again, but instead I said, "You are a disgusting little boy!" and whipped around to walk out of the gym and get out of there.

But, you know, the possibility of a clean getaway never crossed my mind until I turned around and saw that the Polish guy and the weight-trainer guy had halted their "smell me" argument in order to watch the crazy fat-ankle lady at her best, yelling at the small, little boys behind the glass who were at the Y for an educational day of summer camp and telling them how repugnant they were; the receptionist was staring at me, mouth agape, while her phone went crazy; and no eyes were on the daytime talk show, *and there were midgets on.* Nope, all eyes were on me, StairMaster, rowing machine, treadmill, everyone on the real bikes. Me.

Looking at me.

I really did think for a minute about explaining the situation, about how it had all started so innocent and nice and fresh and then the next thing I knew, the little boy had turned into Ron Jeremy and I felt like I was in a Vivid video and before it was over I had flipped off a child I had clearly mistaken for a nearly grown man, I really did. I thought about that.

But in probably what was my wisest idea of the day, I abandoned that thought and headed straight for the locker room, where I opened my locker, grabbed my stuff, noticed three aberrant pubic hairs near the sink, and then fled, never to return.

And that is how I ended up in Sears seriously considering spending my Europe money on a treadmill—not that I had actually planned on going to Europe on $800, but thought that if I mentioned it enough times to the seventeen-year-old salesman he might take pity on me and give me a deal.

"It's just sooo much money," I whined again.

"Why don't you just join another Y?" the sales kid said. "There's more than one in this town, you know."

I shook my head. "I heard something about posters being put up," I said quietly. "Apparently, there are cameras at the Y."

"Well, I don't want to pressure you, but I'm going on break in ten minutes," the sales kid said.

"Fine," I said. "Fine, fine, I'll take it. You worked for that commission, I'll tell you!"

"You could have done the same thing with a priest," he commented.

"When can I get the treadmill delivered?" I asked, eager to get back on schedule.

"Next week looks good," he replied.

"Perfect," I agreed. "Here's the credit card. But before I go, could you point me to the big-screen TVs?"

Don't You Know Who I Am?

I'm afraid I've been a victim of identity theft.

Apparently, I've been identified as an impotent old man with a weenie the size of a golf pencil who is too cheap to buy cable, has a wife who may be cheating on him, trailer-park credit, an identity that may have been stolen, and many, many maladies.

That's the only explanation I can figure out for the amount of junk e-mail I get on a daily basis hawking bottles of Central American "Vibagra," enlargement accessories for certain body regions promising that "When Your [sic] this BIG they call you MISTER," really cheap mortgage rates, and software promising to find "ANYTHING about ANYBODY!!"

Well, it's the latter I know I'm certainly not purchasing, because if their software was really that good they could have easily discovered that I was not a frustrated man with a limp noodle and past due account at a Rent-to-Own joint; I'm a girl with excessively high blood pressure, a freak show for a family, and a credit rating that has completed rehab who got the same stupid junk mail day after day after day for months. I mean, if they really knew me, if they really cared, I'd be getting junk mail for Anna Nicole Lose-Half-Your-Body pills, medical equipment, a spot on *Jerry Springer*, and anger-management videos.

Not to mention that these spam e-mails are just simply unfair to women. Goddamn it, spam makes me wish I had a penis! With all of these irresistible offers served up to me on a plate, I WANT A PENIS NOW!!!! Day after day after day I am taunted by the fact that God left one off of me and decided to give me a stupid, worthless uterus instead. How lucky the penis-bearing population is to be able to take advantage of such incredible offers as "Nothing to lose; inches to gain!!" and offers to "Make Your TOOL a WEAPON!" with a massive supply of Honduran "Vibagra" for the unbelievable price of only $79 if purchased from a Central American country with no pharmaceutical quality control. I mean, come on, we like bargains as much as the next guy, you know. How mean is it to flaunt an unbelievable deal in front of a woman's face and know we can't do a thing about it? Honestly, when I see an opportunity to turn my sex pistol into an AK-47 for $79 full well knowing that I can max out my Visa in hopes of Hilton-sister sex experience that is never gonna happen, that is nothing less than tragic. There in my inbox are deals simply too good to pass up, yet I must, *yet I must*. I want to be called MISTER, my inner penis wants to shout, I want to be that BIG!!!

Now, I've changed my e-mail address no less than six times, have a Yahoo account for the sole purpose of registration purposes on websites, and still, *still*, the spammers find me. It's nothing short of CIA-level sleuthing, I swear, and because of that I'm amazed that Osama bin Laden still hasn't been located. I mean, really, if that bearded bundle of joy has a laptop and access to a Hotmail account, there's a guy out there *somewhere* who's trying to sell him a mammoth-sized evildoer winky and knows where he is.

The thing I have trouble with the most is that with any endeavor, if there are no takers, there's no business, which means that someone is anxiously waiting by his mailbox at this very minute for a package addressed to "They call him MISTER." Once again, it's the bottom of the barrel that ruins it for everybody, as exemplified by the popularity of the still-on-the-air sitcom *Yes, Dear,* NASCAR, Julia Roberts, and the return of leg warmers as an accessory.

Who is buying this stuff? Frankly, I like to think I know a red flag when I see one, but an offer to take out a thirty-year loan with someone who spells their chosen profession as "morgich" would be akin to not only seeing a red flag, but seeing a red flag with the word "SUKKER" pitifully scrawled across it. Can anyone tell me why on earth I would even consider buying a satellite-TV descrambler from a spammer named Rusty Hooker, or "City Lips," an exciting new alternative to getting collagen lip injections that actually "makes your lips grow!!" My lips can't *grow!* I could probably stretch them with the frame of a satellite dish or take out a second morgich for some plastic surgery, but my lips are not redwoods. They've reached their white-girl, paper-thin potential and they aren't getting any bigger on their own until the rest of my teeth fall out. And then there's my ultimate favorite, an irresistible, once-in-a-lifetime chance to purchase the "Most Effective Spam Filter on the Market Today!" Spammers have filled the thin, narrow space in mankind somewhere in between crystal meth dealers and the Bush administration. Honestly, on the evolutionary scale, crack dealers have a higher scum status, since they generally don't come into your house trying to sell you stuff unless you call them first, and spammers rank higher than our government because after you give them your money, at least there's a chance that you *might actually* get a satellite dish in the mail.

Most of us just highlight, click, and delete, that's true, but that's also caused spammers to get crafty and creative with strategies to make us look. You see, if direct e-mail marketers can't get your attention in the subject line of an e-mail by promising to make you a millionaire while you work at home, if they can't force you to look twice in the hope that you will lose seventy pounds in a month with a magic diet pill, if they can't lure you to double-click by tempting you with sultry ladies in the buff, well, then they'll just do the next best thing.

They'll become your best friend. Literally.

For a while there, I was even getting spam from myself. I've received several spam e-mails from "laurienotaro," and unless I'm sleepwalking at night and hoofing it to another job or have a multiple personality inhabiting my body who is selling sex-instruction videotapes as a livelihood, something smells a little stinky, and for once it's not my dog, despite her new "sensitive stomach" food.

Surely, someone would have to be pretty desperate to want to impersonate ME. I'm past due on my digital cable bill, get caught singing in the car all the time, and it looks as if my diet is beginning to wear off and I'm almost able to fit into my fat clothes again. I don't even want to be me! Aside from that, why would I send myself an e-mail when I could just tell myself the same thing and shave that many keystrokes off of my eventual onset of carpal tunnel syndrome? Besides, I *know me*, and if I'm selling instructional sex tapes, you'd do yourself a favor by keeping that credit card in your wallet. I can't fool me! I happen to know that you could probably get better tips looking at cave paintings than watching a dirty movie with me in it. Honestly, I think the only people that spammers can fool with this trick of sending you e-mail with your own name on it is Naomi Campbell and maybe Elizabeth Hurley, who would probably squeal with delight that someone so fabulous, popular, and beautiful would be e-mailing them in the first place.

I don't know how they found me, but the merchants of smut were after me with a vengeance. Somehow my home e-mail address had landed on a list that I was sure was compiled by chunky women with massive red up-dos à la *Gunsmoke* and wearing nothing but see-through negligees and high-heeled slippers with tufts of feathers on them. I really can't figure out how my name got there, since I am a devout subscriber to the theory that if you're going to waste time looking at porn on the Internet, it's best to use work time for that, and since I'm unemployed, it's useless if I'm not on the clock.

I have to admit, when I first began receiving dirty e-mails, I was slightly amused at the colorful subject lines. That novelty, however, quickly lost its entertainment value when I soon started getting ten to fifteen nasty e-mails a day and the novelty was replaced with words even I gasped at. I was grossed out, and then I realized that I was also, sadly, powerless. I mean, honestly, what can you do about it? Who was I going to contact to stop it? And besides, even if I could find the smut peddler himself, it was highly doubtful that a person who puts bread on the table by pushing "Hot, Nasty Teenage Sluts" was really going to pay attention to my priggish little e-mail requesting to be removed from his mailing list, if he would be so kind.

So I adapted my "Plan B For Life" to the situation, which is if you can't fix something, eradicate it or shame it into subversion, then ignore it. And I got very good at it, so good that if I saw a word that I wouldn't even mutter without six or seven margaritas pulsing through my bloodstream, I sent it into e-mail limbo without a second thought. Bink! Bink! Bink! I'd send the obscenities off to cyberspace, all the while careful that I didn't erase an important message from my seven-year-old nephew, who promised to e-mail me from his vacation at Disney World. On one particular afternoon, I was treated to eight steamy messages, and as I highlighted the entire block for disposal, I nearly did the unthinkable.

There, sandwiched between "Horny Sorority Ladies" and "Watch Hot Amy Shower," was "Hi From Sno White and the Seven Dwarfs."

I was furious that my nephew was surrounded by such filth, and I kept on shaking my head and uttering obscenities of my own as I clicked on my nephew's letter to read what he was up to at Disney World. I sure hope what I saw wasn't it. There was "Sno" White, all right, but there was way more than seven little men, all engaged, or about to be, in a very alternate version of "hi-ho, hi-ho, it's off to work we go." They were in places that midgets should never be, particularly Dopey, who looked like he was taking the brunt of the workload.

It was chilling.

It was far too unclean to ignore.

So I developed my "Plan C For Life," which now consists of firing any service provider I pay and hiring their competition instead. I finally changed not only my e-mail address but my Internet provider. I had prevailed over porno.

And when I checked my new e-mail for the first time, imagine the look on my face when I got a message from Sno White and her band of tiny perverts saying "Hi."

Campaign of Terror

"Now you listen to me and you listen good," I said to the girl on the other end of the phone line. "Believe me, you don't want to mess with the Campaign of Terror!"

I could almost hear her trembling in the silence on the other end. It was definitely trembling—that, or she was chewing gum.

"I want my treadmill!" I asserted. "And I want it tomorrow!"

More silence.

"Campaign of Terror!" I threatened again.

"Hold, please," the girl said dryly, and a Journey rock block came over the line.

All I wanted was my treadmill. That's all. After my doctor had informed me that I had gained more weight than an Atkins devotee who takes a bite of a dinner roll, and I could no longer attend my local YMCA because I'd made lewd gestures to a child, I took a second mortgage out on my house and bought sports equipment. After burning approximately three calories on it, I heard a "clink," which developed into a rattle, which then matured into a full-fledged scream. The next thing I knew I was flying backward across the room, though most of the skin from the left side of my body remained on the rubber conveyor belt.

I called Sears. They promised to bring a new one out in two days.

They lied.

When the new treadmill didn't arrive and night began to fall, my husband shrunk back into a corner as I furiously flipped through the phone book. "You know what this means, don't you?" I uttered loudly at no one in particular.

"Campaign of Terror?" he said quietly as his eyes rolled.

"CAMPAIGN OF TERROR!" I confirmed as I grabbed the phone and dialed the number to Sears.

The Campaign of Terror is the method of psychological warfare I invented for dealing with incompetent and ineffective customer-service people, which basically translates into THE WHOLE WORLD. I developed it several years ago while trying to get a refund for work done on my refrigerator by an inept and possibly mainstreamed repairman—also, coincidentally, from Sears. Though he demonstrated an enthusiastic effort to correct my overheated freezer with a screwdriver and hair dryer, both of which he borrowed from me, I had my doubts. Taking his word that the fridge was now fixed, I suspiciously handed over a $112 check with the words "If the ice maker breaks, perhaps we should try a perm."

And so, when the freezer proved to remain broken, the Campaign of Terror was born—out of rage, fury, revenge, and the need to get my money back because I borrowed it from my mom.

Step One in executing the Campaign of Terror: "Greasing the Pig." Be polite and kind, mainly to gain the trust of your vile opponent. Explain the situation carefully and nicely. Then strike with a pleasant, yet firm "I'm sure you folks can easily solve this problem," even though you are aware that the entire population of Mayberry is employed by the company you are calling and Ernest T. Bass is the president. Don't expect a solution; it is far too early and you haven't inflicted enough pain yet. Step One will almost inevitably end with the words of Barney saying, "I'll have a supervisor call you," which has as much meaning behind it as "Officer, I only had *one* beer."

Step Two: "Fly on a Turd." Get the direct number of the supervisor before you hang up. This is VITAL. Otherwise, it's just like waiting for a boy to call you, and before you know it, you wake up and you're eighty with your privates shriveled up to the size of a raisin and able to tie your boobs into a pretzel knot. Give them a window of one hour to call you back, and when time is up, start dialing. Call every fifteen minutes until you get through. Step Two can be *very* effective if you are recently unemployed or have just broken up with somebody.

Step Three: "Verbal Tornado." Remember the motto of the Campaign of Terror and repeat it to yourself and the supervisor: "Nothing is impossible. Everything is negotiable. If you aren't capable of solving this, I'll move on to *your* supervisor, then *their* supervisor, and then *their* supervisor, until I have wasted thousands of dollars in your company's time and someone from upstairs calls *you* and says, 'Why can't you handle a hundred-and-twelve-dollar problem? Get this lady off my back! That moron tried to fix her freezer with a twelve-hundred-watt Conair!' " A special touch here, for seasoned pros only, is to mention "I'm recently divorced and rage is bubbling in a bottomless pit inside of me."

I was just about to mention my recent fake divorce when the customer-service girl put me on hold and my dog started to bark. My husband peeked around the corner and then winced.

"Goober and Gomer are here," he said. "And it looks like they're carrying a boat. Oh, wait. That's a treadmill."

"Ma'am?" the girl said, returning to the line.

"Never mind!" I said as I slammed down the phone and then pointed at the front door. "You see, honey? Another victory for the Campaign of Terror!"

Moving Day

Nana's house looked small and weird.

My husband and I looked around Nana's empty house. It was all gone. The only thing that remained was a roll of paper towels on the counter, and the outlines etched deep in the carpet where Nana's furniture used to be.

"I think that's everything," my husband said as the moving van pulled away from the curb outside.

For more than thirty years Nana had lived in that house, basically ever since we had moved from Brooklyn to Phoenix.

It was, however, time for Nana to go. The neighborhood had started to turn sour, and considering that my eighty-seven-year-old Nana still lived on her own after my Pop Pop had died, everybody agreed it would be best to get her closer to family, so when a house on my parents' block came up for sale, my father jumped on it.

Still, even though Nana's new house was beautiful and she would be far closer to family, it was sad to see her old house empty and alone. I had spent a lot of my childhood in that house, and although we once all lived in that neighborhood, Nana was the last holdout. One by one, we had all moved—myself, my parents, my sister, and now Nana. I had been trying desperately to get her out of that house for years, but looking at her empty living room,

I realized that after it was gone, the last place that our old family memories lived in would be gone, too.

It was a bit unsettling, I have to admit, to see something that was so much a part of my life and my past belong to someone else. I had felt that way when our family home wasn't our family's home anymore, too, but when the house I had grown up in went up for sale, I couldn't blame anybody.

My sister Lisa and her husband had been living in that house after my parents moved, several years before, and, quite frankly, the neighborhood had changed, just as Nana's had.

Gradually, the old neighbors started moving away. They sold their houses to people who let their yards go, didn't water their trees, and who considered their front yards as an extension of their living room, hauling out couches, chairs, and tables and just leaving them there until the weeds eventually masked their presence.

For me, it was rather sad to see our neighborhood disintegrate like that. For my sister, who still lived in it, it was a test of faith. Directly across the street, her new neighbor had been mowing the lawn when the motor seized; apparently discouraged by the unfortunate event, he had simply given up and left the lawn mower to rust dead in its tracks, where it still sat six months later.

The folks who lived in the house behind Lisa developed something of a chicken farm on their patio, which for a rural couple may seem quaint, but when you're living a block away from a major freeway it's a little disturbing, especially on one occasion when a nasty chicken chased my sister down the alley while she was taking out the trash.

I suppose the last straw in Lisa's patience was when the neighbor next door to the Chicken People dragged home a dilapidated railroad car, parked it in his backyard, and used it as a tool shed. Although my sister quickly added two feet to the height of the fence in her backyard, the damage was done and a FOR SALE sign was about to be spiked into the front lawn where I used to do cart-wheels under the huge olive trees.

When she told me that the house had sold, I was both relieved and happy for her, but I wasn't really sad. It was just a house, after all, and now it was a house in a crappy neighborhood. On the day Lisa moved, I went over to help out and was standing in the empty kitchen, staring at the Z Brick my father had slapped onto the walls in the mid-seventies, when it hit me.

We were losing our house. OUR HOUSE.

Our house, where up against that wall my mom used to lie on the couch with her hand over her eyes because she got a headache in 1972 that never went away.

Our house, where, in that same spot, I came home drunk for the first time at sixteen, and despite the fact that I had vomit up my nose and my unfortunate friend Doug had to hold me up with both his arms, my mother *insisted* I was "spaced out on LSD" and demanded that I confess. I guess she was too busy giving birth in the sixties to know any better.

Outside the side door is a small walkway to the carport, where I fled on my tenth birthday during a life-changing event that marked me forever and I won the Most Ungrateful Person, Child, or Adult the Universe Has Ever Seen Award.

I thought my Nana and Pop Pop were going to get me my own TV, for they had indicated as much, and I felt so liberated from the plebeian television-viewing habits of my family that in preparation I walked down to Circle K and bought my own damn TV *Guide*. With a pink highlighter I carefully marked all the shows I could watch in complete and utter freedom, as my ten-year-old life no longer held any obstacles to my delighting in *Little House on the Prairie* alone and in private, or the *Battle of the Network Stars*, when I could cheer on Ma Ingalls without my sister's comments that Jaclyn Smith was going to kick her butt.

But when I opened the package on my birthday, there in my hands was no TV, but a light-blue Lady Remington electric razor, despite the fact that at the time I was still wearing undershirts. Honestly, I don't know what sort of reaction I was supposed to have as I unwrapped the razor—was I supposed to be happy that I was about to sprout more hair than a silverback? Was I supposed to be thrilled that my childhood ended the moment I tore off the wrapping paper, or that the magnitude of my Nana's folly would haunt me for a lifetime? Was I supposed to understand that an electric razor was supposed to make me feel grown up when all I really wanted to do was watch Little House on the Prairie with absolutely no interruptions?

I WAS TEN.

I ran out of the house, threw myself on the sidewalk, and promptly bawled my eyes out. My dad came out and sat next to me. He had already taught me important lessons in my short life, because although I believe my self-loathing, low self-esteem, and manic-depressive tendencies stem from my mother's side of the family, my antisocial behaviors and general intolerance of humanity come straight from my dad, wrapped like a slice of bacon around a filet mignon, in these words of wisdom:

- Ninety-five percent of the people you meet will be complete idiots. Find the other 5 percent and stick to them like glue. Even if they don't agree that you're in the 5 percent.
- Anyone who doesn't agree with you is an idiot.
- Any boss who fires you is an idiot.
- Most of the people you work with will be idiots.
- There should be an Idiot Jail.
- Everyone is trying to rip you off because they think you're an idiot.
- Never buy anything in a dented box.

The biggest lesson, however, came on that sidewalk when he sat with me and said, after a while, "You can't always get what you want. But sometimes, you get your knees." When I mentioned that I already HAD knees, he added, "Yeah, but when you get old they go. And . . . then you really want them back." It was a good effort in rock-and-roll wisdom, but my dad probably should have stuck with the Beatles, whose lyrics were much easier to understand than those of the Rolling Stones. So I learned right then and there that if you're going to quote a song, you better get it right, otherwise you look kind of like an idiot.

Anyway, when it got dark inside, I went back to my house and threw the razor away while no one was looking.

As a point of interest, and as a side note, I didn't lose my Most Ungrateful title until several years ago, when someone beat me hands down. (This will be funny in just a minute.)

It turns out that the first guy to ever have a hand transplant turned out to be an ex-con from New Zealand, and when people found out he had served time in prison, it caused a big brouhaha. Well, not only was he completely undeserving of the handout (I told you it would be funny), but a short while after the transplant he said he didn't even LIKE his new hand and wanted it chopped off again. "I've become mentally detached from it," the New Zealander said in an interview with a British newspaper that I read, cut out, and framed, adding that he realized later that it wasn't his hand after all.

I can't believe he was that big of a loser and I had never dated him. Statistically that's impossible, but in any case, I think my mother needed to take a crack at him. "You'd better use that hand and you'd better like it!" I can imagine her screaming. "So what if it doesn't look like your other hand? You know, there are veterans in Europe who would KILL to have a hand like that!"

And then he'd get a beating.

So apparently, some dead guy gave up his dead hand for absolutely nothing, not even a thank-you. At least my Nana got a thank-you after my mother dragged me to the phone by my hair the next morning after my birthday.

"You're welcome," Nana said. "And don't come crying to me when you start to get all fuzzy and you don't understand what's going on! That's what you get for throwing away a perfectly good electric razor! You know there are women in Italy who would KILL to have a razor like that!"

Down the hall is my bedroom, where, during a freak-out fit of child anger, Lisa, then eight, blew a hole through the door with her foot when she discovered I cooked and ate her last E-Z Bake Oven cake. Hey, it was chocolate and I was thirteen and meeting my hormones for the first time. I was an uncontrollable monster, crazed by chocolate, who would eat anything brown that was in my path, and this included a crumb particle of what looked like a fudge-dipped macaroon but instead turned out to be a dropping of Cycle 3 for fat dogs.

Across the hall is her room, where, as a fourth-grader, she cried for nearly seven hours straight after my mother gave her a home perm that made her look like a Harlem Globetrotter.

The next door is my parents' room, where she stood one Sunday morning, screaming at age five, "OPEN UP, MOMMY! WHY IS THE DOOR LOCKED? WHO IS GOING TO GET ME MY SUGAR SMACKS? UNLOCK THE DOOR!!!!"

Across the hall was my other sister's room, into which she ran after a particularly gruesome fight, slamming the door so hard that it broke the lock and we had to call my Uncle Jimmy to disassemble the window to let her out.

The backyard marks the spot where I taught Lisa, then in eighth grade, how to smoke, to make up for eating her E-Z Bake Oven cake. I lit it for her, told her to suck super hard and hold it as long as she could. Three seconds later, she threw up in the grass.

I smiled. She's a nonsmoker.

It's also the same place that my other sister pinched me with lobster strength and taunted me until I picked up a dried-up, nearly white dog turd and hit her in the leg with it, upon which she immediately threw up, ran to her bedroom, and slammed the door, which resulted in the call to Uncle Jimmy.

On the other side of the yard is the swimming pool, into which Lisa, then a nine-year-old full-fledged spaz, rode her bike, at the deep end, because she couldn't see past her huge perm head.

In the corner of the yard is a fig tree, sturdy, tall, and massive, producing figs that practically drip honey. My father planted that tree almost thirty years ago and babied it gingerly, from a twelve-inch sprout taken from my great-grandfather's fig tree back in Brooklyn.

On the side of the patio is the storage room, bearing a puke-green door. On the inside face of that door, in pencil, are the names of myself and my two sisters, and hatch marks that document how we grew until we all hit our peaks of giantdom at 5'5". Lisa's son at three matched the exact height she was when my dad started measuring.

Our house.

I drove by our house after my sister had sold it. The new owner hadn't moved in, although she had hired people to chop down every tree in the front yard and had rented a massive Dumpster to place the debris of the demolished Z Brick wall and other structurally important elements she was ripping out of the house.

I called Lisa that night and asked her if she thought the new owner had pitched the green door into the Dumpster, too.

"Probably," she sighed. "She called Dad and offered to *sell* it to him. He told me to peek in the alley every now and then to see if it was out there, but I'm too afraid of that damn chicken. It's just a door with some marks on it, you know."

"Yeah, it's just a written-on door," I agreed, nodding, though I understood that we both knew better.

Even now, years and years and years later, when I drive past my old street on my way to Nana's old house, after the Dumpster incident, I can't bring myself to look three houses from the corner and see that house.

Now that Nana was moving, I wouldn't have a reason to drive past it anymore, and I was kind of glad about that. Standing in Nana's empty living room, a different flood of memories came back, memories of my Pop Pop dancing to "Mack the Knife," laughing, yelling that he was a "caged animal in his house" after we took his driver's license away, and the place in the backyard where he would spread all of the old, stale bread to feed a hefty majority of the birds on or about the West Coast.

My grandfather was a character, and we all loved him dearly. I never knew of another grandfather who would do the things he did for me; picked me up every day from school until I finally got my own car; and whenever we went over to visit, he would present me with generic maxi pads and tampons when he found them on a dollar-days sale at Walgreens. He was an avid junk collector, a trash can harvester and pack rat, and he lived by the maxim that one man's garbage was another man's treasure, and the proof was always presented in a sloshy, bubbling Hefty bag, covered in "nothing you can't wash off!" One day, when my mother, my sisters, and I were visiting, he vanished down the hallway and returned carrying a massive cardboard box.

"It's for you people," he said, motioning toward the treasure, in what he could not have known was a tremendous taunt. "It's tonic for your hair. It's brand-name."

My sisters and I ripped into that box like it was filled with E-Z Bake Oven cakes, eager to grab handfuls of Vidal Sassoon, Prell, or the most fantastic bounty possible, the entire line of Fabergé Organics that spelled instant popularity in our respective second-, fifth-, and seventh-grade classes. It was the moment it was actually possible to break away from Notaro Hair, and being that we were traditionally White Rain girls at sixty-nine cents a bottle, we had never had the chance to wrestle free from our cotton-candy hair prison. Our grandfather, we knew, had just made all three of us Charlie's Angels, and, damn it, tomorrow, our hair was going to feather like the back of a duck's ass.

Within seconds, though, the fact that I was blind with possibility and hope vanished, and there it was in the light of truth, as a dozen African-American faces smiled up at us.

"Pop Pop," I said as I tried and failed not to laugh. "This is Jeri Curl. This won't work on us unless Mom slips us drugs, renders us unconscious so that we won't fight back, and gives us home perms again."

"Oh, you don't know!" my grandfather said angrily, throwing up his hands, and snatched the box back. "Hair is hair, anything works on it! You people are just too fancy to use marked-down stuff! Everybody at Walgreens wanted this, you know! The cashier even had her eye on it and tried to talk me out of it, but I knew what she was trying to do. I was thinking! She wanted me to put this stuff back so she could buy it for herself!"

Sure, I felt bad that my Pop Pop had just squandered part of his Social Security check on useless hair products meant for people with a different heritage, and although I loved him a lot, I didn't love him enough to go to school the next day looking like Shalamar or the short guy in Hall and Oates. Furthermore, I could just imagine the look on the cashier's face when the old Italian man shuffled up to the counter with a case of Jeri Curl, could simply not be talked out of his treasure find, and then paid for a case of it.

When I turned sixteen, Pop Pop once again shuffled out of the back bedroom with an oddly and distantly familiar blue box in his hand.

"Here," he said, handing over the Lady Remington from my

tenth birthday, which he had stealthily rescued from the trash years before. "Nana's been using it, but I think you need it more."

The proof of his treasure hunting was in his closet, in his storage room, and in his backyard, where his pilferings from other people's refuse provided the flair in my grandfather's "yard art." Now, I'm not sure what exactly it is about retired men and utterly useless crap that when you introduce the two makes one of them drag the other home and prop it up as a decoration in the backyard. It's not exactly two great tastes that go great together, but rather like the set designer from *Sanford and Son* had stopped by, armed with a van from Goodwill packed with items from a Superfund site. Among his outside treasures were: a Fisher-Price dollhouse, battered and broken, though it proved to be an agreeable perch for the bevy of birds that gathered for the daily feeding, and who, oddly enough, pooped only in the bathroom; Mr. Arizona, as my grandfather named him, an excessively creepy, huge, six-foot-tall stuffed doll that was made, apparently, from an old flag and sat in a chair on the porch; a massive set of bull's horns that he tacked up above the sliding glass door; and a wide, odd variety of ceramic heads that Pop Pop had gathered out of the trash bins of the art class at a middle school where he worked as a janitor after he retired.

The heads were awful, horrible things, ugly enough that either the children who made them were horrified enough of their creations that they threw them away voluntarily or someone with their best interests at heart did it for them. I mean, they were big clay heads, fired and now solid, glazed, painted, and simply hideous; a wonderul idea in theory, but in practice, it was an optimistic assignment with ghoulish results. None of them looked human, they were the stuff of nightmares. I mean, honestly, plop a five-pound block of clay in front of any eleven-year-old and see what you get—it's not going to be the head of the *Venus de Milo* or

Michelangelo's *David*, I can tell you that much. It's going to have honest intentions but wind up more like a disfigured burn victim, a band member from GWAR, or something that escaped from the lab, but that did not stop my grandfather from lining his gardens with them, the grimaces peeking out from behind the bougainvilleas or springing up between the daffodils.

It was, in a word, breathtaking.

If someone were to simply peek over the fence briefly, they might have thought my Pop Pop was Lucretia Borgia or Jeffrey Dahmer, being that the carnage was everywhere, heads, heads, and more heads, and proudly so on display. Pop Pop, however, loved the heads, and even referred to some of them as "cute." It didn't help that they were in an array of colors—green, pink, purple, red, yellow, all easily requisite colors in the spectrum of decomposition, giving the grisly display something of a ghastly, circuslike air.

Over time, their numbers dwindled, as I'm sure some of them broke, but most likely it was my Nana sneaking out to the backyard in the middle of the night to toss them out, slowly, one by one, while my grandfather was sleeping.

After Pop Pop died, they all disappeared, as I knew they would. So did the Fisher Price Poop Bathroom Dollhouse, Mr. Arizona, and the blanket of bread crusts that Pop spread over his grass every day.

Then, one day, when my nephew Nicholas was about three years old, we were throwing a ball back and forth in Nana's backyard when the ball rolled over and stopped at a bush. When I went over to retrieve the ball, I bent down to get it and jerked back when I realized something in the bush was looking at back at me.

There was an eye, a definitely creepy eye, deep in the middle of the bush. I could barely make it out, but it was an eye. I thought to myself that it couldn't be; how could one of the heads be in the middle of this massive bush?

When I looked at the bush closer, I realized it was not really a bush, but the thick, dense shoots of an olive tree that used to be on that spot until Pop Pop had it cut down when I was a kid. There had been a short stump, a stump apparently worthy of becoming a stand for a ceramic creature head, and as the shoots began to grow around it, the head was forgotten, until the shoots became a bush and the head had been swallowed by it.

"There's a head in that bush," I used to delight in telling my nephews to scare the holy crap out of them, and because they were so little I'd get to do it once or twice a year, because they would have forgotten all about the last time I bet them a dollar that Nana had a head in her hedge.

Nicholas, the sensitive, cerebral nephew, would scream and ask how it got in there when I showed him the evidence; David, the aggresive, id-driven nephew, would immediately take a stick and attempt to kill it. Then I'd get to tell them a story about their great-grandfather, whom neither got to meet, and how he used to decorate his backyard with very odd things that made the yard very special. I was going to miss that yard. It was always easy to make a buck there.

It was probably the last time I would be in this backyard. After we moved Nana and got her settled into the new house, there really wouldn't be any reason to come back. Everything was packed, on the truck, and already gone. There wouldn't even be a reason to drive past the house anymore.

In addition, Nana wasn't the only one in our family who was going to be moving. Only the day before, my husband received an acceptance letter to attend graduate school in Oregon. By the end of the summer, our house would be empty, too.

"That's it," my husband said after he loaded the last of Nana's boxes. "We've got everything. We should go and get to Nana's new house before the movers get there."

"Yeah, sure," Nana agreed reluctantly. "Who wants to hang around this old empty house?"

"Hang on a minute," I said as I put my car keys down. "I forgot something."

I went out into the backyard, went to the bush, and stuck my hand in. I was able to get my hand around the face of the head, but I couldn't pull it out from the middle. The bush had been growing for years, and the sprouts were no longer sprouts but branches, some of them an inch thick.

"What are you doing?" my husband said as he came out of the house. "We need to go. The movers can't get in without us."

"Just wait a minute," I said as I stuck my other hand past the branches to the center. "This will just take a minute."

I grabbed the back of the head with my other hand, but I could already tell this was going to be a tough fight. The branches were stronger than I thought they would be, and they had the head in a sort of prison, with the shoots acting like thick bars all the way around it. I just tugged and I pulled; I felt my arms get some deep scratches, but I wanted that head. Finally, I yanked the head out from it's decades-long perch on the stump, through the branches that had hidden it and, in a sense, kept it safe from a Dumpster death at the OCD hands of my Nana.

"What the hell is that?" my husband said, completely horrified. "If that's what I think it is, I did not see this. I didn't. I cannot be an obstructor of justice, I am going to grad school. You lied about your family the whole time! You are just like the Sopranos, but without Little Steven!"

"Touch the grody head," I taunted as I pushed it toward him. "Touch it! And this wasn't a Mafia hit, you dork! It's just the head of my first husband."

"I hate you so much," he replied. "What is that thing? It looks like an Orc. Is that Rosemary's baby, or at least part of it? "

"Naw," I replied, laughing. "It's just my soul."

"Well," he said, "if you won't tell me what it is, would you please tell me what you're going to do with it, and that hopefully it's not going somewhere in our house?"

"Nope, it's not going in our house," I confirmed. "But as soon as we get our new house in Oregon, it's going straight into the backyard."

Back to the Homeland

I swear I am never letting my parents go to Europe again. The last time they went, they came back with roughly nine hundred of the same pictures that everyone who just comes back from Europe has. We were on Photo 765 when my father leaned over the dining room table and pointed to one teeny-tiny minuscule window on the side of an enormous cruise ship.

"Now, that was where we stayed," my father said, tapping the photo with his finger. "See that window? That was the window to our room on the boat. Behind it was your mother, and I think this was in Mallorca, so she stayed in the room and scratched at herself."

"It was a rash, but it was more than a rash," my mother spoke up from the other side of the table. "It was like a full-body scab. It would not surprise me at all if that cruise ship washed its sheets in sand, because when I woke up that first morning, I was nothing more than a tomato with a mouth."

"A tomato with a mouth who vomited every time we hit a wave, which, on a ship, is a little difficult to avoid," my father added.

"That is a lie," my mother replied. "I didn't get seasick until we got to France."

For the benefit of his children and for the trip to Europe, my father invested in an extra-fancy camera that can take wide-angle

180-degree shots, so we "could really get a feel of what it was like," although that feeling could have been reached far more successfully if he had bought us all round-trip tickets to Rome. In any case, my dad had a little trouble figuring out how to use the 180-degree feature, so he basically stood still and clicked, moved a quarter of an inch to the left and clicked, moved another quarter of an inch to the left and clicked, and so on and so on, until he was satisfied after forty minutes that he had captured the whole shot faithfully. That dedication, however, was nothing compared to the time it took to assemble the jigsaw puzzle of the Tyrrhenian Sea my father had thus created and had spread out on my mother's dining room table. For nearly five hours, my entire family was held hostage while my father color-coded specific quadrants of the scene with Post-It notes, unable to leave until we ooohed and aaaahhhed over the finished creation, and individually told him what a good investment the 180-degree camera was. The massive work turned out to be not another boring picture, but another very large boring picture that didn't quite match up in some areas (overexposure was my father's explanation for the gaping holes in the two-foot-by-three-foot image, or maybe it was just the times when he had to reload the camera and forgot in what quadrant he had last taken his quarter-inch picture), which created minor waves of nausea if you looked at it for too long, or, as my mother experienced it, "Makes me feel like France."

"This is Italy," my father said, flipping to Photo 766. "Frankly, I didn't like Italy too much. It was very . . . old-looking."

"At first, I thought the Italians were very friendly and touchy-feely," my mother added. "I thought they could sense we were related, or at one time were one of them—"

"As is documented in Photo 767," I nodded, pointing out a woman whose hand looked disturbingly close to my mom's ass as my mother's sandblasted face attempted to smile for my father's expensive camera but looked more like she had just stepped on a nail.

"Oh, that one," my mother nodded. "I thought she liked me until your father realized she was reaching for my wallet."

"Here," my dad said proudly, "is the Vatican. That's the Pope's window. He sleeps in there. If the light is on, it means he's home. See? The light is ON. You know what that means?"

"If Photo 769 is a shadow of the Pope getting undressed and cameoed by the mystical 'Pope Is Home' light, I am freaking out," I said blankly.

"See this?" my father continued, flipping to another photo. "This is a place called Pompeii where a volcano erupted and covered the town in ash."

"And when they dug the ash out, they found the shells of people laying like this," my mother said as she covered both of her eyes, "like this," she said as she stretched her arm across the table and grimaced, "and like this," she continued, and as she looked up, her mouth fell open and she put her hand to her forehead. "Of course, by the time they were dug out, most of them were dead. Isn't that what the guide said?"

"Something like that," my father said with a nod.

"I think Pompeii was kind of a . . . seedy town," I ventured. "I saw a special on TV that showed some old brothels with dirty pictures on the walls. Did you see anything like that?"

"Pornography was not on my agenda," my mother snapped. "I did not go to Europe to see a peep show and look at filth. Show her more pictures of the Vatican. You wouldn't believe that place if you saw it. The size of that gift shop really is a miracle. It's enormous!"

"Did you bring me back a Pope doll?" I asked eagerly.

"You know who else thinks that's funny?" my mother replied. "People who are turning on rotisserie spits in Hell, that's who. Do you think the Pope's still funny, or do you want to spend eternity as a Boston chicken?"

"Come on, it is *so* funny," I argued. "He could come with a couple of outfits with matching pointy hats, one of those smoky lanterns, and a little tiny lamp with a string you could pull to make it light up and the Pope could say, 'I'm home,' 'I'm not home.' 'I'm home,' 'I'm not home.' "

"Oh, oh, look," my father commanded exitedly and then held up a picture. "Here's France! Here's France!"

"I was so glad to get out of Italy," my mother said. "On our second day there, they fed me a mad cow."

"No one fed you a mad cow, Mom," I said. "You probably just drank some bad water."

"Yeah?" my mother said, shooting me a dirty look. "Water doesn't keep you in the bathroom for seven days and seven nights on a cruise ship. From the likes of what happened to me next, that cow wasn't just mad, it was pissed."

"Wow, look at France," my sister said as she handed me the photo.

I expected to see the Eiffel Tower, Versailles, maybe even the Louvre, but there, in my hand, was a photo of what looked unmistakably like a CVS or Duane Reade.

"Now, France, we liked," my father said as he looked at the picture with me. "This was the place in France where we got Mommy's Imodium A-D."

"Oh, I loved France," my mother added. "That was a good day, a very good day. When I was finally able to go on deck, other people on the cruise told me they thought your father had killed me and thrown me overboard. Some were very worried, even though no one said anything."

It was then that I noticed something odd. In essentially every single photo—with the exception of the one in which my grimacing mother is about to get mugged by a distant relative—the scene or image was framed by what appeared to be red curtains. Not ruling out the possibility that this was the only fancy-pants feature on the expensive camera that my father figured out how to operate, I decided to ask.

"Dad, what's the deal with the red curtains? They're in almost every shot," I asked.

"Oh, those were just the curtains on the tour bus," my father explained. "They're on all of the windows."

"So . . . all of these photos were taken . . . on the bus?" I asked. "The Colosseum, the aqueducts, the Pope's house? The Spanish Steps? You didn't get off the bus? It looks like you saw Europe through a puppet show!"

"Sure, we got off," my mother interjected. "We had to get off the bus so we could get back on the boat! Oh, and in France we got off, too!"

"To get the Imodium A-D?" I suggested weakly.

"I loved France," my mother beamed. "It was a nice drugstore!"

The rest of my parents' pictures weren't any more exciting, to be honest, and frankly, they were just as boring as the pictures I had seen of eight other trips to Europe this year, except that most of my friends who had gone to Europe actually touched the ground. Still, Europe had been "educational" for my parents, as evidenced when my mother commented on an obelisk that "it must have taken a lot of time to make that phallus so big."

I was choking on my own spit when my sister stumbled across the secret stash that was tucked under a place mat.

Pornography, apparently, was written on *someone's* agenda.

Okay, so it wasn't really pornography, just more like ancient-world smut from the part of Pompeii that wasn't rated for family viewing. My dad had apparently stashed them away under a place mat while he handed off the photos of the Vatican and the Spanish Steps that made me more sleepy than the time I took eight Tylenol PMs when I was in a very dramatic mood. In any case, he was keeping all of the exciting pictures to himself, such as the statue of a Roman man with a dinky-doo the size of a car bumper, the frescoes of ladies dancing in the buff, and paintings of what looked like some naked guys wrestling.

"Oh my God," my sister and I giggled as my dad grinned from ear to ear and my mother cried, "What's the big deal? It's just anatomy! Every male has an obelisk! Your father simply took scientific pictures!"

There was an element of biology in them, I'll grant him that, but it was antique porn that I was looking at. My dad had obviously stumbled upon the old Guccione homestead.

I felt my psyche swirl as $3,000 of psychotherapy went right down the drain.

Well, that is, as soon as I got over the amazement that my dad finally figured out how to work the 180-degree feature.

"I thought the colors were pretty," my father insisted.

"Oh, they're colorful, all right," I said. "It's Pompeii's version of the Spice Channel! Some are so dirty, you couldn't even see that kind of stuff on the Spice Channel, they'd have to invent the Dirt Channel just to broadcast it. Did you see this shell of a person, Mom? I don't think he's reaching for his forehead."

"Put those away!" my mother said as my father giggled.

"Did you notice anything odd about those pictures?" he asked.

I nodded. "Yep," I said. "No curtains."

Curse of the Squinky Eye

Bllmmm.

Oh no. No. No. Oh, it can't be. It can't be. Please let it not be.

Bllmmm.

Damn it. *Damn it!* It's my eye, the fluttering eye. That thing it does. *Squinky eye.* It's a goddamn squinky eye. I *haaaaaate* the squinky eye. God, just go away! I hate the way it gets your eye all fluttery, like if just your eye was having a seizure.

Maybe it was a onetime thing, just like a lone squinky-eye eruption, then it will just go back and be dormant.

Bllmmm. Oh God, this is going to drive me crazy. *Drive me crazy.* It feels like a tremor hits the whole side of my face. And I'm supposed to be working. How can I work like this, when I can't concentrate, sitting here, waiting for the squinky eye to hit again?? How I hate the squinky eye!

If I don't think about it maybe it will go away. Maybe I can ignore the squinky eye into submission. Ignore it. Ignore it. I'm ignoring the squinky eye. I don't even understand the squinky eye. I mean, how does it happen? What is going on with my eye that it needs to convulse and then stop? Is it an eye hissy fit? Is it like a skin earthquake? Are the plates of my skull separating, is my face coming apart, is a mountain range being born, or is it just another pore expanding? God, I already have pores the size of pudding cups, that's the last thing I need, another pore I need to fill in with spackle. Flying insects have hit my face and just been swallowed by my pores, never to be seen again, they're like black holes. Why do I have such big pores? I wonder who I should blame for that, my mom or my dad? Oh, my mom for sure. I've never really looked at her pores, but I'll make a point of it next time I see her, I certainly will. Big pores. Thanks, Mom, thanks. As I matured and became an Italian-American woman, my genetic makeup (which for any other culture would be equivalent to a man's) sprang to the fore-front, if you know what I mean. In order to get up the endurance to take a razor to myself these days, I'd have to sleep for three days beforehand to store up enough energy, or consume about a case of Power Bars. Honestly, I think my mother may have taken drugs during all three of her pregnancies to ensure she'd give birth to monkey babies, her own personal insurance policy against any of her daughters becoming strippers.

As if that wasn't enough on my genetics scorecard to push me into another species altogether, but the big hubcap pores, well, they put me right over the top. I wish big pores were hot on a girl. How my life would have been changed. I could plant flowers in mine. If I lay down in a field in Texas, I bet kids would fall into them like a well.

Bllmmm.

Oh, stop it. That's enough, okay, *that is enough.* I wonder if you can see this one, because sometimes you can't. Sometimes you can't, and it's only *you* who knows that your eye is rumbling. Okay, now that I'm in front of the mirror and waiting for it, the squinky eye won't do it. Watch, it won't do it. It will play dead. Come on, squinky eye, come on. I'm waiting for you. Isn't it weird that it happens, like, once a year, and for the whole day you have the squinky eye and then it just vanishes, not to appear until next year? What is it? I wonder if there's documentation on it. I wonder if science has a name for it. I'm so glad I didn't have the squinky eye at my wedding. The pictures would have been merciless— double chin, meatball in my teeth, a twitching eye. Bride with a tic face. My mother should have stopped the whole thing and put me on palsy watch. All I needed was a clubfoot and a stutter and I would have been the perfect hillbilly bride. Maybe it's a probe of some sort that the government placed there when I was born so they could track me, because anywhere that I go, well, there's my eyeball, too. Hell, they could just find me by my pores, they're so enormous they've shown up on satellite images.

Bllmmm. Oh shit. Shit! I wasn't looking. I was looking at that super-long and up until now invisible chin hair. Damn it. Maybe it's some guy pressing a button in some faraway government office to drive me crazy and make me stand in front of a mirror looking at my eye until it freaks out again. I wouldn't doubt that one bit, I really wouldn't. The government does all kinds of crazy things, like dropping LSD in unsuspecting people's drinks in the fifties to see what would happen—they did that. They totally did. I wouldn't be at all surprised if there's a Laurie Notaro Squinky Eye Button and people take turns once a year pressing it. I'll bet it's like popping Bubble Wrap, it loses its fun after about a day, and then it's just boring. I wonder who is pressing mine. Probably an old boss. Or my mom. I would like to press someone's squinky-eye button, I would, I think that would be fun. I wonder whose they'd let me do? I'd ask to do Kelly Ripa, but I bet she's got a list a mile long of people who want to give her a squinky eye. At one squinky eye per year, I bet I'd be dead before my turn came up.

Bllmmm. A-HA! I saw you! GOTCHA! I got you! Saw the whole thing, I saw it contract, make my eye flutter like I was having a stroke, and then vanish. It's a bad squinky, too. . . . God, it's bad. It looks like a fisherman caught my eye with a hook and is tugging on it like I was the biggest catfish he's ever seen. I'm like Oprah in

The Color Purple. It is THAT bad. There can be Discreet Squinky Eye, in which only the person with the squinky eye knows what's going on; it's a very low-key squinky eye and one that understands that a convulsing spasm eye may horrify others and therefore maintains a delicate sense of decorum about the whole situation, but of course I didn't get *that* one. Nope. The one that I have has to look like I have eye epilepsy, because then there are Flagrant Squinky Eyes who don't care who sees them, they are brass and bold and downright mean. They don't care. It's got the whole eye bulging to the bass rhythm of an OutKast song. That's what I have. A Flagrant Squinky Eye, *the overachiever.* It looks like an unborn twin attempting to escape.

I have to go to the store in a little while and I don't want to go if I have the squinky eye. I don't want to be in the frozen food section and have the person next to me freak out because it looks like I've got an alien about to burst through my face and escape through the air duct system—either that, or people will think it's contagious. I can't go, especially because now I know it's a Flagrant Squinky Eye. If it was the lighter version, I could handle it, I could maybe hide it with hair or my glasses, but this thing looks like someone hooked it up to a Taser. I hate the Flagrant Squinky Eye—the Discreet one, well, you can forgive it, it's only doing its job, as far as spasms go, but the Flagrant one just has to push it over the top, like a convulsion isn't a convulsion unless everyone in line sees it and is rightfully disgusted by it. I don't want to stand next to someone with a beating, throbbing eye. Who would?

Blllmmm. JESUS!!! Stop it. Blllmmm. STOP IT. Someone must stop the squinky eye. If they can devote lab space to figuring out that a shot of bacteria will smooth out your wrinkles, can someone please designate a countertop and a microscope to solving the squinky-eye puzzle? Please?

You know, with all the things science has accomplished—they can transplant lungs and kidneys, make babies in glass dishes, clone things—why can't somebody fix the squinky eye? Doesn't it plague humanity enough? At any one given second in the day, I bet a million or more people are all being tortured by the Squinky Eye Syndrome. Can no one stop the squinky eye? Is it that all-powerful? If science can sew a severed hand back onto an ex-con—I mean, if they can develop a pill to give a man an erection for four hours—why does the squinky-eye issue go unresolved? And that's a stupid pill, I'll tell you. I'm sure it seems all fun and cool for the first fifteen minutes, but when it's all said and done, you have to spend the rest of the day indoors and just pray your little boner out that your house doesn't catch on fire. If science can clone me, fix the *goddamned squinky eye*. Really, though, I hope no one clones me. What a nightmare. I believe every baby deserves a fresh, clean slate, you know? I mean, how do you tell a tiny little baby clone who's been Xeroxed off like a company memo that informs people that wiping bad things on the bathroom stall walls WILL NOT BE TOLERATED, "Get ready, Laurie 2.0, it's going to be a bumpy ride."

How do you look at your little clone and say, "You know, when you're five and go on that field trip when you walk into the light pole and your dress flies up after you're knocked unconscious and the whole class sees your panties, just laugh with them when you wake up, okay? It's way better than crying so hard that you throw up, and besides, if you show them that you also find the nickname 'Whorie Laurie' humorous, maybe they won't insist on singing it every time they see you."

When she cuts her first tooth, how can you bring yourself to mention, "Start sucking those choppers in, little sister, or you're going to end up with the overbite of a donkey that can only be marginally repaired by four years of orthodontia, including seven months of round-the-clock headgear after Dr. Ovens catches you cheating on your headgear hourly scorecard."

When she laughs that cute little baby laugh, how can you not begin weeping as you advise, "Boy, after the number that high school does on you, it will take a fifth of JD for you to emit so much as a giggle."

And then—then—there's the gargantuan pores that are so big, people think I must be an overzealous body piercer in recovery.

And who am I kidding, it's not only Laurie 2.0 who would suffer, this clone thing would also suck for me. It would be like dying the longest death possible, watching your life flash before your eyes in real time. Talk about torture! I'd rather have things burned off of me than relive most of the moments from my life, unless I was sleeping, and some of those are pretty humiliating, too.

I'm sorry, but I think that every life deserves to start out, at least for the first thirty seconds, scar-free. Without a full set of emotional baggage. With a clean plate, free of any issues except hunger and intestinal gas. With at least an inkling of hope. You can clone all the sheep you want. I mean, what problems do sheep have? I'm going to eat, I'm going to get shaved, and then I'm going to meet a man with a very large knife. That is *nothing* compared to letting a stoner chick look for a piece of gum in your eighth-grade purse and watching helplessly as she finds the maxi pad flag.

A man with a big knife would have been a godsend.

Hey.

Hey.

I think it stopped. I think it's gone.

Is it gone?

I think it's gone. Or it's sleeping. It's gone or it's sleeping. I don't know. Can't tell.

Oh my God. I think it's gone. Squinky eye? Squinky eye, are you there?

I think it's gone. I think it may be gone. I think it may be safe to go to the store now, because really, a squinky eye is only a little better than having a relentless erection. Really, I mean, how can you go out into public when your whole face is hiccuping? My mind has triumphed over my eye! God, my mind must be power-ful. Well, *duh*. I mean, I kept thinking over and over and over for years that Froot Loops should have marshmallows in them, and THAT finally happened, too, and they come in monster shapes to boot. Finally, it's the perfect cereal, just like I said. *Just like I said.* I predicted it. No, I *made* it happen. Okay, I'm going to pick up my car keys very carefully so as to not wake the squinky eye in case it's resting, and I'm going to go out the door and get into the car. You know, though, it's weird, once the squink goes away, you kind of realize that in a way, you sort of liked it. And sort of miss it. In a very weird way, it almost feels, well, a little bit cool.

Bllmmm.

Last Night at Long Wong's

When I took two steps into the bar and looked down at the stage, my heart broke into a million pieces. The stage was naked, the tables around it empty, and some chairs were stacked, while others sat scattered in random positions.

It was dark, and up near the stage it was quiet.

It was the last night of Long Wong's. In about an hour it would close for good, targeted for demolition in the upcoming weeks. As I stood in that room, I understood it had always been small, but now, for some reason it looked modest, tiny, impossibly little.

My living room, I realized, was bigger.

I had spent years of my life in this place, formative years when I was just starting out as a writer with a column in a college newspaper. I survived on $70 a week but lived off of my friends' generosity; Nikki, one of my best friends and a Long Wong's waitress, would slip me extra wings when I bought a dozen during happy hour; whichever friend's band was playing that night would be kind enough to put me on the guest list so I never paid a cover; Sara, the bartender and another of my best friends, always had a JD and Coke ready for me at the bar when I came in. Then there would be an after-hours party, usually at my friend Patti's place, which was an old, run-down apartment in a tiny 1960s-era complex mere feet from the train tracks, close enough to the bar that you could walk there after it closed.

It was the kind of place where you didn't just become a regular, you became part of a group, a densely packed, oftentimes incestuous community—almost a clique but too big to really be considered one. Everyone knew everybody, and if you didn't really know them, you knew of them.

It was my friend Brian who initially "brought me in" to Long Wong's; he was the bassist in a band that my friend and fellow reporter at the newspaper was doing a story on, and I tagged along for one of their shows. Brian and I hit it off, became great friends, and there I was at Long Wong's, meeting his girlfriend, Nikki, the bartender, Sara, and many of his other friends who soon became mine. These were the same friends I was walking down Mill Avenue with toward Long Wong's one night, drunk and laughing, when one of us made a comment that we were silly idiots, and I chimed in, "We're not just idiots. We're the Idiot Girls' Action-Adventure Club!"

It seemed like we spent a million nights in that bar, eating wings, laughing, making eyes at cute boys who later turned out to be girls, watching our friends' bands play, watching some of our friends get famous, watching their record go gold. Watching the one who started that band get left behind because of a drinking problem, hearing that he had deservedly punched the singer in the face on Christmas Eve, watching the band fizzle out without him.

It was the place where I spent some of the last nights of that friend's life with him, smoking, still drinking, and then him screaming for the bartender on duty to change the station when his own song came on the radio over the speakers.

It was the place where I waited when I got stood up by the same guy again and again because I never sobered up long enough to not take his calls; the place I ran to when I saw the same guy, then my boyfriend, drive away to Seattle with my stereo in a van driven by his ex-girlfriend; the place where I saw my husband for the first time, and the place where I dropped a drink on his foot when he told me I was pretty.

It was the kind of place that, even more than a decade later, I could walk into at any time of the day or night and know someone. People just kept coming back; it was not just a watering hole but a watering home of sorts, a place where you could point to a corner and say, "Remember when Dave Bouchard hurled on the bar?" or "Remember when Doug Hopkins rammed the neck of his guitar into the ceiling?" or "Remember the night when a hippie put an iguana on your head and it shit in your hair?"

Not to say that in all of that time, Mill Avenue—the street that the building that housed Long Wong's had sat on for over a hundred years—hadn't changed. What was once a charming, vintage street with old storefronts occupied by indie record stores, diners, antique stores, independent bookstores, and two handfuls of music venues had been torn down and rebuilt again as million-dollar lofts, home to a Hooters, Gap, Aveda, and McDonald's. In fact, the street that was once an ugly but super-friendly stepsister had, with the help of developers and a lynch mob of chain restaurants, turned into a flashy debutante. A retail swan.

From above, flying into Phoenix from the east, in a jumble of blue, red, and green lights, Mill Avenue looked like a Disney train wreck that interrupted the humble luminescence of the surrounding areas. It wasn't the same place that had been a bigger part of my life than the house I went into to pass out at night.

It's not that I oppose "progress," it's just that in the course of my lifetime, I've learned a thing or two. I've learned that it's better to eat an overdone steak at a restaurant than one that's been spit on, it's never a wise idea to wear a dress if appearing on *The Jerry Springer Show,* and that whenever you find something that you think is pretty cool, it's only a matter of time before someone comes along to ruin it.

Now, granted, the Mill Avenue I haunted wasn't the mecca of

financial prosperity it is today. You could walk up and down the three-block stretch and see at least twenty of your friends. Panhandlers and street kids were years away from hustling college kids and businesspeople for a buck. Back then they only asked for spare change. There was no such thing as a block party on New Year's Eve, or a giant, teetering tortilla chip that plummeted into an immense bowl of fake salsa when the clock struck twelve, sponsored, of course, by Tostitos.

It was when Mill Avenue was still cool. It was a small but devoted community. It was real.

After I married that guy I met at Long Wong's and started hanging out at home on Friday nights, eating movie theater butter microwave popcorn instead of seeing a band at a bar, it had been a couple of years since I'd been down to Mill. I had heard and read about the goings-on in Tempe but hadn't been brave enough to see it until the night my husband decided to take a shortcut.

And I saw it for myself. As we drove slowly down the avenue, through the valley of neon and reflective towers of glass, I hardly recognized it. I scanned the faces of the people on the sidewalks but didn't see one that I knew. Then we passed an ultra-hip restaurant in an ultra-hip, newly constructed building, and as I looked at it with my mouth hanging open, I realized I couldn't remember what used to be there.

I guess although I didn't haunt Mill Avenue anymore, I kind of counted on it to haunt me whenever I felt a little lonely for the old stomping grounds, whenever I wanted to remember the things I was terrified that I would forget.

And now, it was time for Long Wong's to serve itself up in the name of progress. We all knew it was a matter of time, and the lease of the building was up.

Sara, now the manager, threw a shindig for Long Wong's departure. The parking lot was cleared and two stages were set up; bands from my day and beyond were scheduled to play.

This time, I had the ten bucks for the cover charge, and as soon as I went in, I met old friends I hadn't seen in years, people I threw up in front of, people I sat up until sunrise laughing with, people who had moved across the country and came back for this night, people who would pick me up at the airport every time I came back from running away, people I took care of when they were in trouble, people who took care of me, and people who still owed me a drink. People it felt good to see.

I noticed after I had been there for a while that a place looks different if you know it's the last time you're ever going to see it. Long Wong's looked legendary that night, as I remembered all of the things that had happened there, all of the people I met there, and all of the people I saw for the last time there. Sometimes a building is just a building, but even with its rotting pipes, wobbling toilets, and unintentionally springy floor, that place wasn't just a building; it was a base camp. I had always counted on it to be there when I wanted to come home and see my old friends who knew me and liked me no matter what, but in another way, it held the stage for many things that I missed dearly and would give anything to have back. There's something about a place that has your history heavily wrapped up in it that makes it hard to let go, and I had always felt that way about this place, even after I had stopped hanging out there every night. I always knew it was there, and I found great comfort in it—and felt great obligation to it as well. Sometimes, when all you have of something or someone is the memory, the place where those memories were created ties you to it, sometimes tightly, and makes it hard to go too far from it.

At the same time it stood stoutly with a legendary air, it also seemed vulnerable and shoddy around the edges, almost like a devoted dog that was being dropped off at the pound. When I decided it was time to go home, I knew I wanted to see inside one more time before I left for good. I was standing near the stage, where my friends' bands used to play as we would crowd into the tiny place to watch them. I bet I sat in every single one of these chairs, I thought to myself as I looked around, alone, and I was giggling to myself when someone tapped me on the shoulder.

"This is a restricted area," one of the security staff Sara had hired said to me in a voice I knew had to be seven octaves lower than his real voice. "You'll have to leave."

"That's fine," I said, as I looked around one last time, then started up the steps to the bar area. I had just reached the top when I felt another tap on the shoulder.

"Christ, I'm leaving, okay?" I snapped as I turned around, and there was a someone I hadn't seen in almost ten years.

My friend Tom. A friend, something more than that—sometimes where you draw the line is a little fuzzy, and it was with us, too. We were close friends for a long time, as he was one of Brian's roommates and I spent a lot of time at their house, mostly mornings waking up and trying to find my car keys. Tom was a good friend. A really good friend. But things changed and suddenly another girl appeared who paid him attention and was prettier than me, so the whole thing ended badly. We hadn't talked or seen each other since.

"Oh my God," I said, stunned. "Wow."

"I'm so glad to see you," he said as we met in a mutual hug. "We should get a drink!"

We had only been at the bar for a little while when the lights flashed and people were being herded out by the rent-a-cops.

"I'm not leaving," Tom said as he grabbed my arm and sat me back down on the bar stool. "And neither are you."

I laughed, finished the rest of my drink.

"I still have the whole set of luggage I bought with the Marlboro Miles I got from picking up all of the empty cigarette packs in your car," he laughed. "One time I picked up eighty of them on the passenger side alone! It took hours to find them all in that filthy car of yours, and it's amazing I didn't catch a staph infection just from breathing in there. That car should have been condemned!"

"Screw you," I replied. "I'm the one who made the investment. I smoked all of those packs! All you had to do was cut them out and send them in. All I ever got from that was a keychain and discolored teeth. I could brush my teeth with Soft Scrub and they'd still be Marlboro yellow!"

"TIME TO GO!" the bartender, someone I didn't know, yelled again, and this time we didn't have a choice of whether we were staying or not. As "security" (the bald, morbidly obese fake-voice man and a toothpick of a used-up woman who looked like a chicken nervously guarding her sole egg) pushed from the back, we sat as long as humanly possible, but when it came down to the wire, both Tom and I reluctantly got up after the crowd had passed.

"Let's GO! LET'S GO!" the security guard yelled, and I had to laugh.

"I never thought I'd spend my last moments at Wong's being chased by Baby Huey in an 'Event Staff' shirt," I said as they pushed us along, out through the bar, into the restaurant, and through the main door, and as Tom and I walked through it, we smiled. We were the very last two people, ever, in history, to be kicked out of Long Wong's.

"I liked that," I said. "This was a good ending. I'm glad we finally got one."

We walked through the huge crowd that had gathered in the parking lot and said our good-byes to whomever we saw, and I pulled out my car keys to get ready to go.

"Whoa. You two. Is the fistfight over? Did I miss it?" Brian said when we ran into him, and we laughed. "Patti's having an after-hours party! What's a night at Wong's without an after-hours party?"

"A night when I won't have to find the number of a divorce lawyer in the morning," I replied. "I'm old. I'm tired. Tonight I broke my five-year record of staying up past *Saturday Night Live*."

"You're not old, you're dead," Brian replied. "The Laurie Notaro I know would either have to be in the back of a cop car or unconscious to miss an after-hours party. Let's go, it's only one-thirty, the night is still young. Last night at Wong's, Laurie. Last night. You should go."

Patti's party wouldn't be at his shit-hole apartment, however; it would be at the house he bought a couple of years ago, around the corner from the apartment, where his now-wife was famous for putting on quite a spread.

I was debating whether or not I should go; I was content with having seen everyone, and with the way I had said my good-byes. Besides, my husband was home, waiting for me, and I had to get up early the next morning to pack boxes.

"Naw. I have a big day tomorrow," I told him. "I have to finish packing up the kitchen."

"Why are you moving to Oregon?" Brian responded with disgust. "No one knows you there."

Tom begged off, too, and we headed off to where he had parked his bike and I had parked my car.

It really was great to see him. I had always felt horrible about the way things concluded all those years ago, and I waved as he rode away, albeit a bit wobbly, on his bike because he had an inkling he might not have been in any condition to drive by the night's end.

"God, we *have* gotten old," I called.

When I got to my car, I already had my keys in my hand, and I flipped through the ring to find the one belonging to the car. I flipped through it once, twice, three times before I realized it was really missing and the split ring it had been attached to was gaping open and oddly bent.

Oh shit, I thought to myself as I started to panic, it's gone. It's gone. For the first time in a decade I'm sober enough to drive after leaving the bar and I can't find the goddamn key and it's late and my husband is sleeping and I'll have to call a cab and I don't have enough cash for that—it would be at least a thirty-dollar fare. Shit, oh shit. It had to have fallen out in my purse.

I dumped the entire contents of my purse on the ground next to my car and searched through it all like I was panning for gold. The key was gone. I shoved everything quickly back into my bag and ran up the steps of the parking garage, back to the street level that exited right across from Long Wong's parking lot, hoping I could get a ride to Patti's party, where I could figure out how to get home.

The parking lot was empty. In the same place where hundreds of people were milling about only ten minutes before, now there wasn't a soul around. The parking lot was eerily empty, even the security guards had vanished. It was creepy and quiet, and I decided the only thing I could do was retrace my steps in the hope that I might find my missing car key somewhere on the ground, though I doubted it. If it had fallen on the street or sidewalk, I knew I would have heard it.

I scanned the ground all the way back to Wong's, looking for anything shiny, when suddenly a car whipped around the corner, breaking the silence and shining its headlights on me in the dark.

It was Brian.

"I lost my car key," I explained frantically as I stood next to his driver's-side window. "Can you believe it? It's just gone from the ring, it fell off."

"You're never going to find it," Brian predicted. "Where do you think you lost it?"

"God, I don't know," I said, exasperated. "It's just gone. What am I going to do? I'll never get home."

"Get in and I'll take you to Patti's," Brian offered, and I agreed. Just as I stepped back to walk around to the other side of the car, I saw a reflection in a puddle that had gathered in a small pothole.

I reached down into the water and felt it, hoping it wasn't a shard of glass.

"It's my key," I said as I showed Brian.

"Bullshit," Brian replied.

"It's my key," I insisted. "This is my key. I found my key. I can't believe it. Can you believe it?"

"That's really your key?" he asked, eyebrows raised.

"Absolutely," I nodded.

"So do you want to go to Patti's or not?" he asked. "Everyone's there."

"You know," I said, thinking about it, "I think I'll just see you guys later."

"All right," he said. "Last night at Wong's . . . ?"

I laughed and I nodded, and then I waved him on, knowing that he was right.

It was the last night.

And so I went home.

My Big Mouth

As soon as I opened my mouth and those awful words came tumbling out, I knew I had made a horrible mistake.

Even I couldn't believe what I just said.

So far, Nana, my husband, and I were having a nice lunch at an outdoor, cozy little Mexican restaurant on the outskirts of Phoenix. On the little pond in the center of the restaurant, a new mama duck glided about peacefully, her ducklings behind her as they swam from side to side.

Everyone was having a wonderful time, mainly because everyone loves ducks, particularly baby ones. Baby ducks, recipients of love from the world at large, baby ducks. Who doesn't love baby ducks?

I do. Loooooove baby ducks. I have never eaten one, so I had no residual guilt shrouding me. Not a hunter. Never hit one with my car. Don't even own a mallard. I am openly disgusted when I see them hanging in a Chinese market, and am apt to even create a big deal over it, making small, but audible, gagging sounds.

Looooove ducks. Especially the baby ones.

And so did our waitress, who, after serving us our entrees minutes before, stopped at our table, gazed out the window onto the pond, and just stared, somewhat sorrowfully, I might add, as her eyes drooped, her eyebrows lifted slightly, and the smallest, teeniest, yet still visible tremble possessed her upper lip. Now, at first, no one said anything, probably for a good several minutes, mainly because we were hoping she'd just go away. The three of us—myself, Nana, and my husband—just went on eating our meals, saying nothing, each individually thinking that it was weird that the waitress had turned to stone at our table.

"Is something wrong?" I finally asked, because it was quite clear the waitress wasn't going anywhere, and eating dinner with a stranger lurking above your food can make you a little uncomfortable, much like when a hungry homeless person is staring at your soon-to-be-devoured turkey sandwich from the sidewalk and rubbing his belly.

"Oh, no," she replied, jerking herself back into the moment. "No, not really. Well, actually yes, now that you ask, yes. There were nine ducklings this afternoon, then there were eight, and now there are only seven."

"Oh, that's horrible," Nana replied. "Do you think people took them?"

"If only," the waitress sighed. "There are turtles in the pond, too, and I think they . . . I, well, I think they got two ducklings."

The forkful of chicken chimichanga I just put in my mouth sank there like dead duckling as I struggled with the thought of chewing it. Then the three of us slowly turned toward the pond, and that's when I saw it.

"Oh, no," I cried. "There. Look there! Yep, you're right, that spot on the pond right there looks like a little collection of feathers. Tiny little feathers, because I'm sure turtles don't eat feathers or they came loose in the attack, because from the looks of things it was rather violent. Oh. That's so sad. It's just a watery, floating little grave. Poor little duckling."

I turned back to see three faces staring at me, each frozen in true, explicit, naked horror.

No one said anything. They just stared.

"Didn't you see it?" I asked. "It's right there, where those baby duckling feathers are floating. In a clump. Right . . . there."

And that's when I felt something sharp—and around size thirteen—kick my shin hard and fast and rather painfully under the table and saw my husband motion to the waitress, who now had both of her hands covering her mouth, which, though hidden, was obviously in the shape of a soundless scream. She looked something like the Edvard Munch painting, but with permed blond hair and fake sparkly gems imbedded in her fingernails.

Her eyes gleamed like huge diamonds with all of the tears that had gathered in them.

It was then that I realized what I had done.

"Oh, wait!" I said, pointing toward the ducklings' watery grave again. "Look at that! Clearly, I am a moron! Those are leaves! THOSE ARE LEAVES! And twigs and . . . puffy, fuzzy . . . pieces of a . . . a . . . feather pillow . . . maybe . . . probably . . . that's not in any way the grisly remains of a baby duckling, it simply is not. It is not. I can assure you of that. It's just a big collection of stuff that looks like bones and feathers, that's all. Now that the sun has moved and I see it clearly, that can't be a duckling carcass. It simply cannot. I must be drunk."

I turned back around just in time to see our waitress run from our table to places unknown.

"You are an idiot," my husband said frankly. "You are an idiot."

"I need more iced tea," Nana notified me. "And that one is never coming back. Can I have your water?"

"Why did you say that?" my husband asked me. "What the hell made you say that?"

The truth was, I had no idea. I really didn't. I saw what I saw and I reported it, simple as that, without straining it through the sensitivity-appropriateness filter at all. It all just came gushing out at once.

"Maybe I just had a stroke," I offered up. "I don't know! It just came out, I couldn't help it. I mean, I saw those feathers and I just . . . said it. I mean, she was wondering where they went, and, well . . . there it is."

"Those ARE leaves, you jackass," my husband said. "But now that you told the waitress it's a 'watery grave,' she'll never believe you."

"Oh, whatever," I said, and then pointed to the clump of whatever it was floating on top of the skeevy pond. "That's a dead baby duck body and you know it!"

"There's a dead duck in the pond?" I heard an older man sitting at the next table ask his waiter.

"Iced tea," Nana called to anyone, holding up her glass.

Well, I really was hoping that the dead-duckling event was an isolated incident, but as it turns out, it was merely a foreshadowing of events yet to occur. I had apparently, or at least temporarily, lost control of my mouth, and it was running rampant, attacking innocent people all over the countryside. Even though I have an evil little goblin named "Shut the Shit Up, You Asshole" that lives inside my head and makes me yell at people in traffic and when they park like shit, I am, believe it or not, typically able to stop myself before I say something horribly wrong. Suddenly, I was unable to stop what was coming out of my mouth or push the edit button. It was completely unsettling, especially because I had recently been on the receiving end of a similar situation myself. The weekend before, I had been in Oregon to try and find a house. Naturally, I arrived on the hottest day of the year, a very ripe 103 degrees and 90 percent humidity. It was ghastly. My innards had been steamed so effectively I was nothing short of a walking pot sticker, and since I couldn't check into the bed and breakfast I was staying at until four P.M., I got off the plane, drove around for several hours, and looked at houses until the magic hour arrived. By the time I rolled in the front door of the cutest, most perfect Victorian house that was oozing with deliberate charm, my shirt was pleated so extensively that my torso looked like an accordion as I breathed in and out. My ring around the armpits was nothing short of mortifying and hadn't been seen in civilized parts since pioneer times, unless you count chain gangs, and my makeup had long since vanished into the folds of my neck as a constant stream of unrelenting sweat diluted whatever attractiveness factor I may have started out with that morning. I was a sweaty, messy, nasty, smelly wreck of a girl, and my thighs were sticking together. Whatever portions of my hair that weren't soaking wet flew wildly about like live snakes, as I had neglected to weigh them down with pennies or anchors. When the delightful, impeccably groomed innkeeper, who was absolutely, undoubtedly not perspiring in the least, saw me standing in her perfect *House Beautiful*–caliber foyer, which typically received only *House Beautiful*–caliber guests, I believe her initial beauty queen reaction was to point me toward the nearest soup kitchen, but I cut her off at the pass to avoid making the situation any more therapy-worthy than it already was.

"I'm Laurie," I said too cheerfully. "We spoke on the phone last week. I'm staying here for two nights."

"Oh," she finally said, obviously taken aback, her hand at her throat. "We . . . I . . . I thought . . . you would be . . ."

She didn't need to say it. It was written all over her dry, matte face.

"I know," I finished for her. "You thought I would be prettier."

So you see, I knew the danger that verbal shrapnel caused,

and I knew it was not something to be taken lightly. Within a matter of days after the duckling incident, however, it had happened again.

Now, I must explain that across the street from my house is, to put it nicely, a friggin' cat farm. A filthy, disgusting, smelly, reeking, repulsive, feral cat farm, manned by none other than the Cat Lady, as the entire neighborhood knows her. There are so many cats it actually is more appropriate to call them a herd, and, in polite terms, we've begun to reference them not as the diseased, flea-infested pathetically neglected animals living in squalor that they are, but as "free-range kitties."

We have so many cats, in fact, that when I heard that scientists had picked cats as the next animals to clone, I had to take a Tylenol PM and drain the nearly crystallized remains of a mudslide bottle from our 2002 Christmas party, the only liquor we had in the house.

I mean, WHY?

Cats? Why are we cloning *cats?* Who picked *cats?* Is there anyone out there who thinks the world is running a little short on cats? Don't get the wrong idea, it's not that I hate cats, because I don't, I even have one, but I have to be honest and say that the reason I even have him is because there's too many of them OUT THERE.

You know, I have to wonder how this happened in the first place. At the cloning place, do all the cloners gather around and throw scraps of paper with their favorite animal in the hat and whatever is written on the piece that the boss draws is what science is going to clone next? I can just see the faces of the genetic engineers who wrote down things like "Wooly mammoth," "Albino tiger," or even "Sasquatch," on their slips of paper, only to have the big boss pull his hand out of the hat, unfold the scrap, stare for a moment, and then quietly utter, "Cats."

There would be an uproar.

"Cats?" the other scientists would yell. "Why are we doing *cats*? You know, after we pulled out 'mice' the last time, I TOLD you we shouldn't let Sheila vote anymore!"

And then, slowly, all eyes would turn to the corner of the room, where Sheila, the fifty-two-year-old, graying single mother of Mr. Mustache, Mai Tai, EddyPuss, Banjo, Jessica Fletcher, and a sassy Siamese named Earl Grey, presses a bunched-up tissue to her nostril and pulls her balled, acrylic cardigan lab coat tightly around her as the room is overtaken by a sharp kitty chill.

I mean, really, there is no need to make more cats, especially *on purpose*, and I kept mumbling that as I was chewing on my last crystal rocks of mudslide mix. Some of the things I've personally witnessed are so *wrong* that I'm amazed her yard isn't enveloped by fire and brimstone. You want cats, I'll *give you cats*. I've got one-of-a-kind collector's-edition cats with one eye, three ears, one nostril, one leg longer than the other, half a tail, no tail, stump for a tail, you want it, I can get it for you. My block has the market cornered on free-range cats. And we get a whole new crop several times a year, too. When they're not eating, they're pooping in my yard and peeing under my house, which is the same place they go when they feel like dying.

So no, I don't think we need to be constructing, assembling, building, fabricating, or Xeroxing any more damn cats. WE HAVE ENOUGH CATS. REALLY. We don't need copy cats.

My new neighbor, Meghan, also decided that we had enough producers at our local cat-cloning factory, and since she still had the energy of a new neighborhood resident and had not yet experienced the brutal disillusionment that I had, she took action. She located an organization that would come and trap the cats, take them to a clinic to get them fixed, then drop them back off at the Cat Farm once everything was all over.

Cat Lady agreed that it was all right with her as long as it didn't cost her anything, and one evening, the cat-nappers came, set up traps all night long, and took the kitties away. Suddenly, it was like a real neighborhood, well, except for the picnic table in the Cat Lady's front yard that served as a pyramid-like perch for those vermin-ridden cats all day long, and now that it was unoccupied, the Cat Lady invited her family over for a barbecue, and then they sat around the unwashed Cat Table and gobbled up everything on their plates, aware or unaware, I don't know, that they were essentially eating on kitty ass.

I licked out what was left in the mudslide bottle, and I swear everything I ate that day tasted like cat turd.

The day after that, the cats came back, one by one, and one by one they sobered up and climbed back onto the Cat Pyramid, minus their reproductive organs, which, personally, I found absolutely delightful, realizing I would never again be kept awake by the wanton wails of thirty cats in heat demanding to be serviced. I also delighted in knowing that although the Cat Lady fed the cats, which enabled them to live in their diseased states *longer*, she really didn't believe in caring for them, so with the death rate at typically one or two a month, I figured that within a year, our block would be free-range kitty FREE.

Meghan was curious about how many cats the cat-nappers had nabbed, and, to be honest, so was I, because I wanted to work out my Free-Range Kitty Mortality Rate Sheet in more precise figures. When the Cat Lady came out for that evening's feeding, we went over to the gate to talk to her.

The Cat Lady shook her head. "Well, they didn't get *all* of them," she told us with a sigh, as if she was bothered by errant cats peeing and laying turds in her yard as much as we were. "A couple of them stuck around, and then I found one of them dead in the neighbor's yard, right there. It was horrible!"

"Oh, that's too bad," Meghan said, to which I nodded. "What happened?"

"Well, I'm not real sure," the Cat Lady started with another sigh and went on to explain that when she went over to pick it up with a shovel and a piece of cardboard, it was lying with all four legs and the tail sticking straight out from its body.

I do believe I visibly cringed. Disgust, I have found, has no manners.

"But then," the Cat Lady said with yet another sigh, "I remembered that sometimes, dogs will chase down a cat and try to kill it by sitting on it and suffocating it. That must be what happened. A dog sat on it and pushed the air right out."

Now, although I was wrestling with both the visual of a Corgi holding down the claws of a crazed rabid cat with its paws and attempting to sit on it, in addition to the overwhelming temptation to step forward, slap her on the side of the head and scream, "You are insane!" then step forward, hit her again, and scream, "God, you are *completely* insane!" I somehow did not.

Instead, I shook my head and said, "Oh, I don't think that's the way it happened, but then again, you really don't want to know what I think happened to that cat."

"Oh, what?" the Cat Lady implored, looking mildly concerned.

"Well," I began, and then took a deep breath. "What I think happened to that cat is that a tweaker was walking by here on the way to the park up the street to go buy some crystal, picked up your cat by the tail, twirled it around his head a couple times, then threw it."

The Cat Lady didn't say anything, but, déjà vu, I had seen that face merely days before on a teary, weepy waitress who never did come back to fill up our iced teas.

"Oh, you really don't think so!" the Cat Lady cried from behind the hands that were covering her mouth as her voice cracked. "You really don't think that's what happened!"

I looked blankly at her, because even though I sure as shit did— but considering the damage I had done at the restaurant (I mean, really, we were thirsty throughout most of our meal)—I needed to fix what I had done.

"No," I said flatly. "A dog totally sat on your cat."

I was confessing all of this to my therapist when she abruptly choked on a sip of coffee.

"Wait—" she said as she held her hand out and coughed, then burst into a gunfire of uncontrollable, full-throated laughter. "Wait a minute. She thought a dog *sat* on her cat?"

"Can you believe that?" I agreed. "It was more plausible for a dog to have sat on her cat until it was dead than to have a crazed drug fiend kill it a block away from Crack Park. I mean, how did the dog know the cat was dead? Did he put a little doggie mirror in front of the kitty's mouth?"

My therapist, who looks just like Sigourney Weaver, continued to laugh, wiping tears from her eyes.

I absolutely adore my therapist. Every other week, I go and hang out, we chat, we laugh, just like girlfriends over coffee, except at the end, I write her a check for the hour we've just hung out. Sure, it's the closest thing a married straight girl can do to hiring an escort, except that she never has to tell me that I'm sexy, just funny and not as insane as my mother likes to tell people. And she likes to see me. I think she really looks forward to our visits. I'm her favorite. I am.

I *am*.

"How did the dog know when to get up?" I continued. "If they don't know it's not bacon, how do they know the cat's not still alive?"

She laughed again. "You're so funny!" she said.

"Thank you." I blushed.

"So this blurting out . . ." my therapist said. "Is this something you think we need to work on?"

"Hell, no." I smiled. "It's like my own little version of Tourette's syndrome. I'm beginning to like it. It's so . . . liberating. You should see the looks on people's faces. It's priceless, really."

"You are so funny!" she said with a smile and a short, little shake of the head.

"Thank you." I blushed.

"Maybe we should work on your catastrophic tendencies today?" she asked.

I waved my hand. "What's the point?" I asked. "I watched *60 Minutes* on Sunday, and soon as I get it mastered, terrorists will park a dirty bomb outside my house."

"Funny, funny!" she giggled as she waved her finger at me.

"I'm hungry," I blurted out. "You know, you should really think about setting up some sort of snack bar in here. You could put a soda fountain right on that file cabinet and get a hot dog roaster for your desk. Like after our 'time together' is up, you could put on a visor, apron, and see-through gloves and have a business on the side."

"That's hysterical!" she agreed, slapping her knee.

"You could get a homemade cotton-candy machine, I'd love to have that to nibble on while we talk. And fresh roasted peanuts are always a really nice touch," I added. "Chips and dip? That's a party maker right there. And then you could bill it all to Blue Cross/Blue Shield!"

We *both* got a good laugh out of that.

"Oh! Oh! Oh!" I went on, "How about ice cream? You have enough room under your desk for an ice chest, nothing fancy, maybe some waffle cones you could whip up right over here, and of course, Ben and Jerry's and—"

"Time's up," she said quickly with a nice, sweet smile.

"Oh," I said as I smiled back, getting my checkbook out of my purse. "Boy, that went by fast, didn't it?"

She nodded slowly and stood.

"You don't really want to know what I think, do you?" she said, and then opened her office door.

Stretching the Truth

When the uninhibited lady on the couch winked at me, I knew I was in trouble.

There was no way out.

I smiled back hesitantly and then looked around the room nervously. No one had noticed, but there was no way I was engaging in a reciprocal wink.

I was not there to make friends with winking naked people.

I was simply there to paint them.

When I initially signed up for the painting class, I thought it would be a great way to relax and have some fun, perhaps open the door for my inner Monet to pop out and introduce himself. Those hopes, however, were quickly dashed in the newborn moments of becoming a painting student, when, after greeting the class, the instructor simply told us to get out our paints and get to work on the still life he had created on a pedestal.

Sure, I was a little disappointed that it wasn't a vase of roses or modern-day version of Venus, but I was up for a challenge, I decided. I would let my inner artist guide me. I stood there for a moment, waiting for the coffee mug placed next to an antler and a tree seed pod to speak to me, to reveal some sort of hidden inspiration. However, they did not. This presented something of a problem for me, as in "I've seen a lot of things in my house, such as flying mice, a contractor having a nervous breakdown and crying like Nancy Kerrigan in my laundry room, and doors that open by themselves, but, oddly enough, a body part, a cup of decaf, and tree trimmings have never been coupled on my kitchen table, so I'm having a little trouble investing the necessary faith in this supposed still life, particularly because all of the elements in it are very much dead."

I mean, really, had I known that I had just written out a check simply so I could paint somebody's leftover garage-sale junk, I would have saved myself the money, stayed home, and painted the crap on my neighbor's porch. It was equally as idiotic an assemblage, plus there would be a deformed cat or two thrown in for good measure, which is far more entertaining than, say, a dried-up tree pod. That wasn't art, I argued to myself; it looked like a cover shoot for *Guns and Ammo* magazine. All that was missing was the Skoal and a flak jacket.

Needless to say, I was a bit disappointed in the subject matter, but I trudged on with "Antler and Coffee Mug," hoping that somewhere down the line, genius would strike and I would wind up with a realistic representation that would amaze me. That did not happen, either, or at least did not happen insofar as what was on the pedestal was realistically represented in my painting. Instead, my painting would have been much more realistic and impressive if my instructor had drunk the coffee, gone number two on the pedestal, and then suddenly torn his lymph nodes right out of his neck and nestled them by the bottom of the mug.

I sucked. I have seriously met elephants that paint better. My nephew, who, at three, has as much hand-eye coordination as an adult who has fried his brain on crystal meth, had a better grasp on perspective and rendering than I did. I sucked even worse than I thought I would. I sucked so badly it was truly astounding that anyone could be so bad at painting, and had PAID to find out just how bad. That painting class was like going to analysis and having your therapist tell you, "Well, no wonder the world is against you. You are a terrible, horrible, disgusting person, that's why. And you have no talent to speak of. Doy," and then flick you on the head. I wasn't relaxed in painting class, and I wasn't having any fun, either. As if that wasn't bad enough, when I was done with "Turds, Coffee Mug, and Glands," the instructor announced that our paintings would be critiqued by himself and the class.

I bit my tongue, even when I heard the instructor say before the critique, "Now, which painting is the best-accomplished still life, and which painting went in the wrong direction?" I bit my tongue, even when I realized I was the third-suckiest in a class of eight, meaning that two others were even worse at art than I was. Thankfully, I was not crowned Suckiest Painter that day, but I saw the face of the girl who was, and she was no happy Picasso.

"Does anyone have any comments?" our instructor said, after successfully destroying the microscopic art self-esteem the Suckiest Painter had left.

"I stink as a painter," I confessed to the group, figuring that it was just a matter of time before I was identified as the dunce and it was better to get it out in the open and understood immediately. "I know right now that in therapy this week I'm going to need at least forty minutes to talk about the damage that's been done here, and my therapist is out-of-network, so we're talking at least a hundred bucks. Sure it's tax-deductible, but that's almost as much as I paid for this class."

Nobody said a thing.

"Any other comments?" the instructor finally said. "Aside from the negative one we just heard?"

I reluctantly talked myself into going to class the next week, hoping it would be better, but as soon as I arrived, I knew I would be starting on my suckipiece, "Three Ashtrays, a Goblet, and a Juicer—and More Tree Pods."

Although I would, without a doubt, have more fun watching

whiskers grow out of my chin than attempting to bring the soul of the juicer to my canvas, I painted it anyway. When critique time came, however, I raised my hand before my instructor could say anything.

"I have a suggestion," I barreled loudly, completely uncon-cerned that I would be labeled class big mouth, since my outburst last week had clearly identified me as such. "I would really prefer if we renamed this segment of the class 'Although Your Painting Is Already Incredibly Fabulous, Here Are Some Tips to Make It Even More Stunning.' "

"That's a good idea," the second-suckiest painter said quickly, realizing his debut as class loser was probably only moments away, being as his juicer looked more like a gas pump and his ash-trays resembled lumps of toxic waste. The girl who walked away with the Most Untalented honors from last week nodded in agree-ment.

"Well, if that's what you want," the instructor said with a frus-trated sigh, and then continued in a flat voice, "Which of these paintings hit the mark, and which are Fabulous But Would Be Even More Stunning with Some Tips?"

Despite the ground the Sucky Contigent had gained with that modest little victory, success subsequently evaded me in my fu-ture works, "Plastic Ivy in Bowl, Sticks in a Jar, and Yet More Seed Pods," "On Location: Air-Conditioning Unit and Gutters of Build-ing Where Painting Class Is Held," and my favorite, "Parking Lot, a Portrait in Black."

My biggest challenge, however, came the day I arrived for class and a woman with long gray hair I had never seen before was help-ing our teacher move a futon/couch and a fake palm tree to the front of the room.

I set up my easel, palette, and paints and was wondering if maybe the strange lady with the gray hair was some famous artist and a guest speaker for the class. Those suspicions were duly un-raveled, however, when I looked up at the same moment she stepped right out of her dress and sat down on the couch.

Naked.

Now, it's a matter of public record that I do not traditionally do well with naked people, familiar or otherwise. It's just not my thing. I grew up in a Catholic house where naked was a sin of equal proportion to taking a dollar out of the collection plate or thinking that I'd like to date my cousin. You could die for a sin like that, that's why God made lightning, my mother said. But I was older now, I reasoned with myself; plus, after we painted the air-conditioning unit, most of the class called it a day and the sur-vivors left were myself, the girl who was suckier than me, and Carlos, my only friend in the class, but that was mostly due to the fact that he really didn't speak English very well and as a result would laugh at anything I said.

It didn't help matters that the naked lady wasn't exactly an ex-ample of God's divine craftsmanship as far as the human body was concerned. She clearly was not Botticelli's version of Venus. Rather, it would be far more accurate to say that if you were flip-ping through cable channels very late on a weekend night and happened upon a stomach-churning scene of four people getting it on in an above-ground pool during a swingers' weekend in Arkansas on HBO's *Real Sex*, chances are one of them would prob-ably bear a reasonable resemblance to the Gray Lady, give or take a tooth. I have, in fact, seen that very scene, and it has done noth-ing but confirm the fact that the *Real Sex* series is simply a grue-some reminder that other people besides Paris Hilton are out there getting down, too. I'm talking about ugly people, a group from which I am not exempt, although, rest assured, you're not going to see my bare fat ass moaning on a pool pump. *Real Sex* is like the *Red Asphalt* of erotica, it's the part of sex we all know is there but only serves the purpose of shocking you into staying sober for a while to avoid the danger until the horror fades.

Now, believe me, I'm not the sort of person who believes that the female body is only beautiful in the airbrushed pages of *Playboy*, but what I saw before me was astonishing. My first instinct was to immediately run home and marinate myself in potent, skin-firming lotions as I stood there with paintbrush in hand, thinking to myself, *Just how many kids did you have?* I understand that the tug-of-war with gravity is always brutal, but this lady lost it *all*. There was no tug-of-war involved here, it was nothing short of a tractor pull. The stretch marks were actually stretch stripes, but they complemented the scar from an abdominal surgery rather nicely and subtracted a bit from its shock value. The scar was so huge that, personally, I didn't think you could even get scars like that anymore, I mean, it was the kind of scar you would get defending a village against marauders with axes, a disfigurement acquired during a pirate fight, a sentence after being convicted of witchcraft, or something you'd get by living in Africa, but unless she had had frequent exposure to a turbine on this side of civilization, I didn't even see how something of that magnitude could have happened. But she didn't seem to mind at all, and I had to hand it to her. I've made twenty bucks in what I considered the hard way, and that only involved going out to lunch with my mom and keeping the change.

I painted her head first, then the outline of her shoulders and the contours of her body, and then it was time for our first break. The Gray Lady jumped up, threw on her robe, and headed over to Carlos's easel.

"Very nice," she said, looking at his rendering of her.

Carlos laughed. And then he clearly didn't know what to say, because he just stood there, and she just stood there until finally he uttered a phrase I'm sure he had practiced only for going out on Friday and Saturday nights: "Do you work out?"

I choked on my own spit.

Work out? *Work out?* It probably takes half the day just to capture those slinkies into the cups of a bra! Damn you, Carlos! I thought to myself. You should be taking ESL *and* painting! Then you could have asked something good, like "Breast-feeding—was it worth it?" or "So, what did they take out of there? Sextuplets or a tire?"

"Nope," the Gray Lady answered Carlos. "I just do housework, that's how I stay in shape. Vacuuming and dusting, that's my gym! I quit my job to become a model, you know."

Carlos laughed again.

I was seriously doubting Carlos's allegiance to me when the Gray Lady came to my easel and looked at what I was doing.

"My head isn't THAT big!" she commented.

"Oh, I'm not good with heads," I replied. "But if you had a pair of antlers growing out of yours or had seed pods for eyes, I could swing that part."

"Well, you got most of it right," she informed me with a hearty giggle. "Let's see how you do the rest."

She then moved on to the other girl's painting, looked at it, and was still making comments when the instructor announced that the break was over.

The Gray Lady slipped off her robe, settled on the couch again, and we all went back to work. That was when I realized that the part I needed to work on next was the torso area, I began to paint that area as realistically as possible, and that's when I understood I had a problem. I looked at the Gray Lady and looked back at my canvas, and looked at the Gray Lady again and looked at my canvas again, and I just decided that I really needed to do my own thing with the Gray Lady's torso. Not only because it would have looked nicer, but because it was kind. If she came around on our next break as she did on our first, what was I going to say when she remarked, "Why do my boobs look like striped carrots?"

And what could I possibly say to that? "Because, clearly, you were never a Playtex 18-hour girl and you believe gravity to be only a scientific term and not your personal archenemy"?

I already had too much stress in this class, I didn't need to begin offending people who were merely there to take their clothes off for money. If she had a problem with her HEAD, the boobs issue was sure to spark a fistfight.

I looked at the Gray Lady again, and that's when she winked at me.

I decided right then and there that in my world, the Gray Lady was going to fight gravity like it was Tonya Harding with gloves on—and win.

You got it, sister, I thought to myself. I don't care what the teacher says, you are getting a ten-thousand-dollar breast augmentation ON ME!

And boy did she. I traded in her swingin', rock-in-a-sock yams for beautiful, pert apples, firm and round as if she was just plucked from the dawn of puberty. The Gray Lady was on her way to becoming Venus, or at least an employee of Christie's Cabaret wearing a Cousin It wig.

I was working on the left apple when I sensed a presence behind me, and then a hand came out of nowhere.

"Oh this," the hand said, making a circular motion over the more completed apple, "this area is off. It needs to be . . ."

And then the hand dropped six or seven inches, to the Gray Lady's scar area.

". . . down around here."

It was my instructor, and I was caught. The room was drop-dead quiet, so I certainly couldn't explain to him, "Listen, chief. As soon as you call a break, she's going to skip over her to see this painting and that's bad because she thinks she looks good. Got it? She thinks dusting is the same as the StairMaster, and, really, I am not here to pop bubbles, all right? If she thinks her boobs haven't dropped like rotten fruit off a tree, I'm not going to be the one to tell her. Maybe she thinks it's just her cat nestling in her lap when she sits down, but it's not going to be me who gives her the news-flash that it's the girls and that her melons now look like they went through a saltwater taffy pull."

Instead, I looked at him and his rotating hand and simply said, "Okay."

So I moved them down just a bit, a tiny little bit, enough to sat-isfy all three of us, I thought, and I fiddled around with the brush until he came back and shook his fingers in front of the "aug-mented" portion of the painting and said simply, "In this direc-tion. Lower."

I shook my head a little, and kept darting my eyes over to the Gray Lady, trying desperately to communicate to him, "This is the deal, Neal. You picked this lady, and if you want to paint sag on the nag, that is your option. Next time I suggest you take a peek at the twins beforehand and pick someone who's paid attention to the Oil of Olay ads so I don't have to go through this again, be-cause I don't think anyone in this room is going to gain anything by painting flapjacks. Now please let me paint my breasts the way I want to. Please. I have painted your turds, I have painted your glands, I have painted pavement. Can you just let me have this? I, frankly, would rather be painting daisies. What is wrong with a flower? They don't come and peek at your paintings on break. They don't comment, 'Oh, my stem's too long, my petals are too droopy.' I never wanted to paint an old, floppy naked crone with an abundance of scar tissue, that's not art, that means someone sold me a bad hit of acid and I still have an hour and half left on this trip!"

But he wasn't getting my message as clearly as I would have liked and understood my communication to be a seizure or aneurism, so he called a break.

"Maybe you should drink some water," he suggested gingerly.

Before I knew it, the Gray Lady had thrown on her robe and was wandering about, just as I had suspected. I stepped over to Carlos's easel, where she was now stationed, and saw that he had chosen to paint the Gray Lady as if she were underwater, making everything rather blurry, particularly the boobage area.

I nodded my head at his painting as we looked at each other, to which he just shook his head, pointed to his chest, and shrugged.

"Genius!" I mouthed to him over her head.

The next student had clearly moved her easel once she figured out what she was up against, and on her canvas, behind and above a fake potted palm tree, floated the Gray Lady's head. The rest of it was just the tree. Parts of it did, in fact, look like daisies.

When the Gray Lady arrived at my easel, she didn't say anything at first. She stood there for a while, cocking her head to the left and to the right, taking it all in.

"My head is still big," she said blankly. "But the rest of it is . . . uncanny. It's just amazing."

I would have had to agree. It was, by far, the best critique I had ever had.

I nodded and she nodded as we stood in front of the painting.

"Okay, break over, let's return to the pose," the instructor called out.

"The painting is yours," I said. "And keep up with that dusting!"

"Oh, I will," she assured me. "Better than the gym!"

"I hope you come back next week," I said, right before she returned to the couch and the robe slipped down to her feet.

Acknowledgments

Thank you:

Bruce Tracy, for always having time to talk me out of my tree, for being understanding, for being patient, for being honest, and for being an invaluable and incredible friend.

Jenny Bent, the toughest, most amazing girl I know. You are the best and I adore you.

The guy who hasn't divorced me yet, who makes me laugh a million times a day, lets me be the jackass that I am, votes the same way I do, and promises not to commit me for at least another five good years.

Nana, who not only gives me a drawer when I visit, but also gives me "The Big Bed." Never had a better roommate than my Nana, even though she makes me watch a lot of Court TV (new favorite channel). No one rocks like she does. No one. We love you, Nana, you crazy old woman.

My family, um, I live in Oregon now. I gave you back your Tupperware for a reason, because I still wasn't done with it, to tell the truth. Thanks for the material, not writing your own books, and not changing your last name.

Jamie, for making me pee with laughter every time we talk, and for always knowing exactly what I mean (especially when you-know-who is home and I have to whisper). Jeff, for never changing, for taking all of my shit when I moved, and for staying a true, dear friend for multiple decades, but man, your cell phone *still sucks.*

Kelly Kulchak, who is the coolest dork I know, for her endurance, belief in us, and outdorking me EVERY SINGLE GODDAMN DAY. I love you, but not in that way.

Adam Korn, sweet Adam Korn, for still picking up the phone when my number pops up on caller ID (may I say again I think AKorn is funny, but let's just all be glad it's not AHole), and the wickedly addicting Mickey Rolfe, for his fabulous stories and downright impossible good looks. To David Dunton, for keeping my shit straight and babysitting me; and Shari Smiley, Kathy White, and Sonya Rosenfeld for working hard and watching out for me.

Annie Klein (I miss you!); Team Pretty (I am sure I've driven you nuts); Donna Passanante; Nina Graybill; Pamela Cannon; Beth Pearson; Laura Goldin; Kimberly Obitz; Meg Halverson; Bill Hummel; Theresa Cano; Kathy Murillo; Doug Kinne; Sessalee Hensley; Jules Herbert; Craig Browning; Duane Neff; Amy Silverman; Deborah Sussman; Cindy Dasch; Laura Greenberg; Beth Kawasaki; Eric Searleman; Michelle Savoy; Charlie Levy; Patrick and Adrianne Sedillo; Charlie Pabst; Colleen Steinberg; Erica Bernth; Maryn Silverberg; Mary Jo, Henry, and Sylvia at Rosita's; Marie, Becky, and Rhonda from Fairfax; Bill Homuth; Sharon Hise; the Public Library Association; the Arizona Library Association; Scottsdale Library (even if the other authors at the fundraiser thought I was a community-college student doing a research paper and asked me to get them drinks); Changing Hands; and bookstores big and little and their employees, for your wonderful support. To everyone who was SO NICE to me on the last tour, and especially David in SF who took me to Pancho Villa and then stole ice cream with me (that kicked ass).

And then, of course, there's the girls, Kate, Nikki, Sara, Sandra, and Krysti, my wonderful and patient friends. I'm sorry I am the suckiest of them all. I will try to do better.

I'm also sorry to my mother-in-law for hiding from her and eating a candy bar instead of answering the doorbell. I know it wasn't nice and I wish I could promise it won't happen again, but if I don't have a bra on, I won't answer that door if Ed McMahon or Rapture Jesus is knocking on it.

And the biggest, most obnoxious thanks of all goes to all of my pals who have joined the Idiot Girls' Action-Adventure Club, have e-mailed me, have waited months for me to get the kits out (more apologies), have come from near and far to a reading, have stood in line to get their book signed by this asshole girl, and have been so truly, truly kind to me. Idiot Girls kick ass. Every single one. And don't you forget it.

love, laurie n.

About the Author

Under the cover of night, Laurie Notaro ran away from her former home in Phoenix and is now holed up in Eugene, Oregon, a town so nice it took her a remarkable *three whole months* to build up enough anger to flip someone off in traffic. She loves ghost stories and seeing models cry, and is under the impression that she looks cute in hats (sadly, this is not true). Against all odds, this is her fourth book.

About the Type

This book was set in Quadraat Sans, a typeface designed by Fred Smeijers. His first Quadraat typeface was serifed, and he successfully adapted it to a sans version without sacrificing its lively and humane character. Quadraat Sans has display qualities, yet it is efficient, making it equally suitable for texts. Fred Smeijers (born 1961) was educated in typography and graphic design at the Arnhem Academy of Art and Design. He has been designing typefaces since the 1980s.